MASTERING the Art of Personal EVANGELISM

+++++++++++++++++++++++++++++++++++++

HOW TO WITNESS TO ANYONE—FROM ANYWHERE IN THE WORLD—OF ANY BACKGROUND, WITH TOTAL CONFIDENCE AND WITH GREAT SUCCESS.

APOSTLE: PASTOR GLEN E. KERR

Mastering the Art of Personal Evangelism
How to Witness with Total Confidence, and with Great Success
by Apostle: Pastor Glen Kerr

Printed in the United States of America

ISBN 9781613799215

www.xulonpress.com

= Dedication =

This book is respectfully dedicated to the memory of my late sister Bobbette Kerr-Oakley. Since you've been gone, your absence has left a void that cannot be filled. However, we're looking forward with confidence to that grand reunion—you'll never be forgotten.

To my parents: for your dedication, faithfulness and commitment to the service of the Lord.

Words seem inadequate to express my sincere gratitude to you for the extraordinary investment you've made both in my upbringing and your continual prayers and support through the years. The impact of your love, support, and particularly your prayers cannot be overemphasized. I love you both.

To the body of Christ, the ecclesia (the called-out ones), those who are set apart for God's purposes, and most importantly;

To those who are willing and ready to take the message of salvation to the world.

TABLE OF CONTENTS

SECTION 4: HOW TO WITNESS TO DIFFERENT GROUPS OF INDIVDUALS

= Acknowledgements =

First, I would like to give honor to Yeshua, Jesus the Christ, righteous ruler of the earth and giver of life—summed up appropriately in John 10:10: "I come that they may have life and that they may have it even more abundantly."

Special acknowledgment goes to my beautiful daughters Alphia, Fiona, and my adopted daughter Tarasha—and especially Alphia who assisted with her pedantic proof-reading skills.

I would like to acknowledge my very good friend Dionne Bryan for her moral and spiritual support.

My deepest gratitude goes to all the brothers and sisters who labored with me in the gospel, especially those who provide valuable inspiration and support for ministerial engagements.

Special thanks to all the bishops and pastors, around the world, from the United States of America, Africa, Canada, the Caribbean and Europe who shared their pulpits with me. It has been a real honor to be of service to you and your congregations.

And how can I forget the countless number of people, and particularly the young people whose lives have been transformed through the ministry that the Lord has placed in my trust.

It has been my pleasure to see you submit to God, and grow in grace, wisdom, and knowledge of our Lord Jesus Christ.

= Preface =

Did you know that ordinary believers just like you have the capacity, the authority and the power to propagate the world with the gospel of Jesus Christ? Yes, I believe you do. God has equipped you with power from heaven to take the message of salvation from your homes, to your neighborhoods, into your towns and cities and to the uttermost parts of the earth in full confidence and with great success. This is how **Acts 1:8** explains it. "But you shall receive power when the Holy Spirit has come upon you; and you shall be witnesses to Me in Jerusalem, and in all Judea and Samaria, and to the end of the earth." Unfortunately, for most in the body of Christ this has not been our experience.

Recent surveys proved that personal evangelism is not a priority for most 21st-century believers. It's almost like a curse word, guaranteed to drive fear into the hearts of thousands of Christians across the globe whenever it's mentioned. We know we've got good news to share but are doing very little to get the word out—however, I believe that many more people would be involved in witnessing for Christ if they knew how.

God has gifted me with the ability to connect with and share the gospel with people from all walks of life, including scientists, atheists, agnostics, and people from other religious persuasion such as Jews, Muslims, and Hindus to name just a few, and I want to share this gift with you.

In the chapters that follow, I will share techniques, principles and strategies to assist you in fulfilling your duty as a witness for Christ, so you can share effectively and without fear with anyone you meet. We'll discuss obstacles and solutions to solve them. I will also show you how to approach others in confidence, even if you have little or no psychological, philosophical or even theological knowledge.

There are already a number of books on the market on personal evangelism, but most are theological in nature. It is therefore not my intention to give you another lecture on personal evangelism, but rather to provide you with basic step-by-step instructions, and tools to help you become a bold and powerful witness for Christ.

By the time you finish reading this book I believe you will find it far easier to share the good news of salvation. May God bless you and open your eyes to the countless opportunities to change the eternal destiny of those you encounter on a daily basis.

= Introduction =

Becoming a Master of Personal Evangelism

Have you ever wondered why twenty-first century Christians are not having the same impact on the world as did the Early Church? At its inception the Early Church experienced phenomenal growth—in spite of severe persecution. So what accounted for such amazing growth? The fact is, although many were martyred for their faith, they refused to renounce the name of Christ. And their powerful testimony to God's saving power led others to realize that it was actually something worth dying for.

Another reason for this phenomenal growth was that, as a result of the arrest, imprisonment, torture and executions the early Christians fled to safe havens in the region—moving from place to place. From an evangelistic perspective, this was not a bad thing, because they went taking the gospel with them. Truly, even in the case of severe persecution, we can say that "the enemy meant it for evil but God meant it for good."

Persecution is not only an Early Church phenomenon—every year thousands of Christians around the world are persecuted for their faith in Jesus Christ. And as it was in the Early Church, some are even martyred. In 1968 Richard Wurmbrand, founder of Release International (an organization for the voice of persecuted Christians) was powerfully used by God to bring a passionate call to action to the Church in the West from the so-called underground church in Eastern Communist Europe. "Pastor Wurmbrand had been tortured by the Romanian secret police during the cold war years of the 1950s and 1960s. Why? Because he steadfastly refused to bow the knee to communism, and would not compromise his faith in Jesus Christ."

In more recent times the news and other sources have been inundated with reports of ongoing situations involving the persecution of Christians around the world. For example, on January 1, 2011, a suicide bomber killed twenty-three Christians at a church in Egypt; in Colombia: illegal armed groups including the FARC guerrillas assassinate twenty to thirty pastors every year. They make these attacks frequently, targeting pastors and Christians, forcing them to stop preaching, harassing them, making them disappear, and murdering them. On April 7, 2011, a pastor and his fourteen-year-old daughter were murdered outside an evangelical church by right-wing paramilitaries during a Sunday morning service. More than 300 pastors have been killed between 2000 and 2010. They are a target of the illegal armed groups because they promote a faith and lifestyle which directly conflicts with the values and aims of the armed groups. In March 2011: Shahbaz Bhatti, the only Christian minister in Pakistan's government and member of the cabinet was assassinated, accused of criticizing Pakistan's blasphemy laws. In Iran, 282 Christians in thirty-four cities were arrested between June 2010 and March 2011. Many remain in prison while others have been released but only after posting large sums of money. In North Korea even today the freedom of association and freedom of worship and movement are denied. North Korean Christians are forced to worship in secret. Owning a Bible is enough to land them in detention. I could go on giving you instances of persecution of Christians in countries such as Indonesia, India, Ethiopia, Nigeria, Eritrea and the list goes on. What I found amazing though is that despite the persecution, torture and death, these Christians are totally committed to stand up for their faith. This is summed up relevantly by Christian lawyer Jiang Tianyong of

China only two days before being seized by officials. "I am afraid of torture but that cannot stop us doing the right thing."

In the Western world, however, we do not really know what it is to be persecuted, but the truth is, we are nowhere near resolute enough to defend our faith to the death.

These days so-called Christians tend to walk away simply because they feel God has failed to answer their prayers in a timely manner or in the way they expected. We clearly don't have the same urgency and/or passion to reach the lost with the gospel of Christ, as did the early church and indeed, those in other parts of the world where persecution is the order of the day.

Having said that, it's not all bad news, because even now God is raising up a new generation of passionate Christians, a militant Joshua-like generation filled with desire to both claim the promise and to share the good news of the gospel. The thing is, it's going to take the efforts of all of us combined to win the world for Christ, which means those of us sitting on the fence must become proactive, equipping ourselves and asking God to stir up the fire within us.

The question we have to ask ourselves then, is, why is this 21st Century western generation of Christians failing to make that kind of impact on the world?

There are a number of likely reasons for this. For example, many people are fearful when it comes to speaking to others in general and particularly when it comes to sharing their faith. Others may not necessarily be fearful, yet they do not do so on a regular basis. What then, is the problem? Here are a few possibilities. Some may not believe they can effectively share, so they refuse to even try. Others don't believe it's their responsibility to win souls. They think it should be left to those who are called for that purpose. Some aren't even sure there is a hell, and because they aren't convinced, they wonder—what is the point of sharing the gospel? And last but not least are those who simply aren't motivated to tell anyone about Jesus. Perhaps they tried to share and were rejected, and now have little or no confidence to try again.

> "The harvest truly is plentiful, but the laborers are few, therefore pray the Lord of the harvest to send out laborers into the harvest." **Matthew 9:37**

While Christians in the early church were committed to the spread of the gospel, the lack of motivation has probably existed since time began. We know that because in **Matthew 9:37**, Jesus told His disciples: "The harvest truly is plentiful, but the laborers are few, therefore pray the Lord of the harvest to send out laborers into His harvest." He gave a clear mandate to His disciples, which also includes you and I—those who call ourselves Christians. This then would be a good place to begin: we ought to be petitioning heaven asking the Lord to burden us with the urgent need to tell the world about Jesus.

The fact is, there is too much work to be done for anyone to stand idly. Do you remember the parable that Jesus taught us regarding the Landowner who went out hiring workers for his vineyard?

> "For the kingdom of heaven is like a landowner who went out early in the morning to hire laborers for his vineyard. Now when he had agreed with the laborers for a denarius a day, he sent them into his vineyard. And he went out about the third hour and saw others standing idle in the marketplace, and said to them, 'You also go into the vineyard and whatever is right I will give you,' So they went. And again he went out the sixth hour and the ninth hour, and did likewise. And about the eleventh hour he went out and found others standing idle, and said to them, 'why have you been standing here idle all day?' They said to him, 'Because no one hired us.' He said to them, 'You also go into the vineyard and whatever is right you will receive." **Matthew 20:1-7**

Notice the fundamental question in this passage, 'Why have you been standing here idle all day?' And please take note of the answer—'Because no one hired us.' These were probably the rejects—maybe they were looked on as not having the right skill to get the job done, and therefore no one hired them.

Perhaps that has been your situation. You may have been standing idle for a long time because no one anointed and appointed you—maybe for one reason or another they do not believe you are qualified, because you did not have the right educational background etc. It is possible that you are not perceived to be articulate enough and to make matters worse you have bought into that notion.

Maybe you are one of those who are not predisposed to offer your services to the Lord at the appropriate time, or it is possible that you may have been around for a long time and have harbored the thought that you have gone past it—but notice that the master in the parable above went out at the 11th hour of the day—a very unusual hour for hiring people. It is never too late and the reward is the same as those who have started early. In essence, the requirements to be of service to the Lord are not these accolades, its availability—you need only to be available for the master's use. The master of the vineyard simply said, "Go and I will give you what is right."

Remember that a parable is an earthly story with a heavenly meaning. It means then that the parable of the vineyard represents the rearing of souls for the kingdom. God is the master of the vineyard and is still recruiting. The market place is the world, It does not matter how long you have been idle or how old you are. All you have to do is heed the call and go. It is God who calls you to do the work, and promises you will be greatly rewarded.

SECTION 1

Understanding Your Purpose as a Witness for Christ

Chapters 1 - 3

= CHAPTER ONE =

Personal Evangelism A Most Unpopular Christian Ministry

Why is it that most Christians who genuinely love God and attend church regularly are happy to be involved in various church activities and yet when it comes to witnessing, it's a whole different proposition? There is an unprecedented lack of enthusiasm in the area of personal evangelism. Most Christians would rather be entertained or even listen to a lifeless preacher, preaching a lifeless sermon to a lifeless congregation than to listen to a message on evangelism. We all long for our family, friends and sinners in general to come into the knowledge of Christ that somebody once shared with us but to actually tell them about God almost always feels strange.

Statistics show that 95% of all Christians have never won a single soul for Christ, and eighty percent do not witness on a regular basis. Less than 2% are involved in evangelism, and 71% don't contribute toward any evangelistic outreach whatsoever. Most believers are of the opinion that evangelism should be left to those with special gifts, special callings, and special titles. But that is not the case: witnessing is the duty of every believer in Christ.

With no new converts added to their numbers, many churches see no growth for years, and some even close as older attendees age and die with no one to replace them.

It is no secret that Christians can be found all over the world and in practically every place inhabited by people. They are in colleges, places of employment, in industry and sports—you name it and you will find Christians represented. Unfortunately, most of the time they have little or no influence whatever on the lives of those around them. It does not matter where you are; if you are there, God has put you there for a specific purpose—to be a light to reflect the love of Jesus and share the gospel.

Lest you believe otherwise I am well aware of the challenges that arise when witnessing, especially to those in your immediate circle. However, it's a tragedy that many have never even attempted to share the need for salvation with their families, neighbors, friends, fellow students or colleagues.

Even some of those who have been in the church for years and hold positions of influence are often very uncomfortable sharing their faith. The truth is that if we really love the Lord and believe that hell is a real place where unbelievers go for eternity and that without remedy, we should be passionate about sharing the gospel to save them from such a tragic end.

1.1 Lack of Awareness

As I have said earlier, one of the main reasons more Christians are not engaged in personal evangelism is because they do not believe it is their Christian duty to be witnesses. As a result, they simply sit back and do nothing about it. **Hosea 4:6 says**, "My people are destroyed for lack of knowledge."

And then there are those who feel that you shouldn't have to say anything if you live your Christian life in front of others. The trouble with such thinking is that no one is going to learn of their need for salvation by merely looking at your life. In fact, this generation has used that excuse for silence for far too long. Indeed, if you are not communicating by speaking out as a witness for Christ, you are hiding your light under a bushel, where no one can see it. Jesus said, "Let your light so shine before men, that they may see your good works and come to glorify your Father which is in heaven."

The reality is that it's your God-ordained duty to tell others about Jesus and their need for a Savior. **Romans 10:14-17 tells us:**

> How then shall they call on Him in whom they have not believed? And how shall they believe in Him of whom they have not heard? And how shall they hear without a preacher? And how shall they preach unless they are sent? As it is written: How beautiful are the feet of those who preach the gospel of peace, who bring glad tidings of good things. But they have not all obeyed the gospel. For Isaiah says, 'Lord, who has believed our report?'

But here is the big point, verse 17, "So then faith comes by hearing, and hearing by the Word of God." Notice that faith does not come by seeing but by hearing. **Therefore, you must tell them in words**. The fact is, if you don't tell them, they may never hear, and if they have never heard they will spend their eternity in hell—which is a matter of great urgency that should stir your soul like nothing else can.

1.2 Feelings of Unworthiness and/or Guilt

Another reason believers fail to witness is that they feel unworthy and suffer from the guilt and shame of their past. Why does this happen? The Bible says our enemy, Satan, is the accuser of the brethren. He's always pointing an accusing finger at you and reminding you of your past. If guilt and shame describe you let me say here that, though you may have committed the worst sin imaginable in the past—that sin was forgiven the moment you confessed it and asked Jesus to save you. You are not a victim of your past; therefore, you must forgive yourself and move on in full assurance of your new found faith in Christ Jesus. **2 Corinthians 5:17** says: "Old things are passed away, and behold, all things are become new." Glory to God! You are not the person you once were. In fact, instead of feeling guilty and holding on to the vestiges of your past, you should use your testimony as a tool for sharing the gospel to bring others to salvation, fulfilling your God-given destiny and purpose.

1.3 Ashamed to Be Identified with Christ

In my opinion, one of the most unfortunate reasons why Christians do not witness is that they are ashamed to be identified with Christ. For example, many people have been working in the same place for a number of years, yet their work associates do not even know they are Christians.

I hope that if you are not actively involved in personal evangelism, it is not for this reason. No Christian ought to be ashamed of the glorious gospel of Jesus Christ. The apostle Paul tells us in **Romans 1:16 – 17** "For I am not ashamed of the gospel of Christ, for it is the power of God unto salvation, for everyone who believes, for the Jew first and also for the Greek." Verse 17 continues: "For in it the righteousness of God is revealed." In other words, the gospel message is a revelation of the righteousness of God. It goes without saying then, that if the world is to be evangelized, you and I will have to do our part to make it happen.

1.4 Unaware of the Urgency to Reach the World for Christ

Some may be unaware of the urgent need to bring the lost to repentance. They might even argue that they struggle just to keep themselves right with God, so that the spread of the gospel takes a distant backseat to maintaining their personal relationship with God. But that is a poor excuse for letting others die and go to hell. That's much like taking out a personal insurance policy against the fires of hell while paying little or no attention to those who are perishing around you. Scripture says that if we say we love God we are to love our neighbors as ourselves, which means we are to be concerned about their eternal destiny.

As I see it, the real problem is that we have not laid aside our personal agendas to pick up the cross and seek God's heart. As we seek God's heart we will feel His deep sense of urgency to bring souls to Christ, because time is short, and those He loves are dying every day with no one to snatch them back from the edge of hell. Instead, we have bought the notion that Christianity is supposed to be glamorous, performing before spotlights and gathering in vast sums of money. That, however, is the Devil's most devious and clever lie, because it appeals to the lust of our flesh and what we think we want most. If we have swallowed such nonsense we are far from the heart of God, because God sees the unsaved as kidnapped royalty, those He died to save. But do we care? In **John 4:35** Jesus reveals God's heart concerning this matter when He says, "Do you not say, there are still four months and then comes the harvest? Behold I say to you, 'Lift up your eyes and look at the fields, for they are already white for harvest!" He's saying here that we are not to wait for a special call, a personal anointing or a special season, because the time is now and the need is desperate. We don't need more spot-lit stages; we need altars where we can repent of our apathy and intercede for the souls of those who are lost and going to hell.

> "Do you not say, there are still four months and then comes the harvest? Behold I say to you, lift up your eyes and look at the fields, for they are already white and ready for harvest"

It may sound glamorous to be called a pastor, a bishop, an apostle, a worship leader, etc. and stand before crowds, but if you are a disciple of Christ your heart should be heavy with the urgency to see people saved, delivered, healed, and set on fire, living with a passion for Jesus Christ. And whether you believe it or not, it is not just the pastor or the evangelist whom God has called to win the lost. He calls all of us to "Go therefore into all the world and preach the gospel to every creature." **Mark 16:15**

In 2007, the Center of Missional Research conducted a study of over 7,500 master's degree graduates from seven seminaries. Study questions asked how well their studies prepared them for evangelism. Eighty-eight per cent said they felt well-prepared to share the gospel with others. In fact, they felt equipped to evangelize as much as they felt prepared in biblical studies and theology. Because that was the case I found it remarkable to learn that most of them responded that they "do not practice evangelism frequently."

If over 7,500 graduates participated in the study, then more than 6,600 (88%) of them felt adequately prepared to share the gospel and yet most of them did nothing about it. That leads me to conclude that just because someone is well-versed in the methods of evangelism doesn't mean he actually does it. Clearly there is a vast difference between preparedness and the commitment to winning souls.

So what does that mean in real terms? To be blunt it means the church is failing to carry out the Great Commission, and as the study has shown, church leaders are not exempt. This problem exists from pulpit to pew.

While some may argue that the gospel goes out regularly via many avenues, including books, magazines, television, radio, and the Internet, I maintain that there is nothing that compares with a personal, one-on-one gospel witness shared with passion and excitement about the person of Jesus Christ and the need for a Savior.

In our generation we have mistakenly expected people to come to us in the church to hear the gospel, but obviously that effort has been a dismal failure. Why would they come to us when they believe the church has little of value to offer them? It's high time for those of us in the church to set aside our own agendas and take to the streets, getting involved in peoples' lives, to demonstrate the love of Jesus in practical ways.

Again I must emphasize that, barring an emergency where they are desperate for help, unbelievers will rarely ever darken the door of a church, especially if they know no one and have no connections there.

At this point you may argue that you know of many fast-growing churches. But what if I were to tell you that most fast-growing churches are made up of church hoppers—those, who move from church to church in search of quick and easy answers to difficult life situations and also for personal gain? One study reported that only 15% of churches in the United States are growing. Out of this, only 1% is added to the church because they were newly converted by the power of God. The other 14% are church hoppers—a disastrous state of affairs, to say the least.

1.5 Lack of Preparation

It takes preparation to impact the world for Christ. That means we must change our thinking about what it means to share the gospel.

According to Brent Price of the ***New Spirit Filled Life Bible* (NKJV)** on the subject of personal evangelism,

> "The present post-modern era is vastly removed from times when God was commonly at the core of human thinking about life, made manifest through architecture, art, music, and literature, and seriously considered in philosophical thought. But a fundamental change has occurred. So much of society, impressed with its achievement, has gradually crowded God out of a central place in thought and values. Still, the reality is that human nature hungers for God, and thereby many people cultivate private pursuits for Him on their own terms, inevitably becoming confused about spiritual reality."

It's clear that we no longer center our lives around the things of God, and we no longer possess the readiness of heart and mind to change the world for Christ, though there is an urgent call to return to that place.

1.6 Lack of Conviction

I believe that we as the body of Christ is experiencing a crisis in several key areas—among them are a lack of conviction about the urgent need for the gospel, and our level of confidence in the Word of God. By that I mean, if we do not have full confidence in God's Word and our faith in God, we won't be able to sell such a notion to anyone else. It's no different than a salesman who has no confidence in his product. No matter how much effort he puts into it he will not be able to influence many people to invest in his business—in fact, he is bound to be a dismal failure at his trade.

Whether they look like it or not, those around you are desperately hungry for the truth, something solid and unchanging to believe in and count on. Though most will not admit it to those around them they are searching for answers to the tough questions they face. Internet sites such as the New Age, Eastern mysticism and even Satanism sectors are inundated with hits by those looking for answers. But they will find only confusion there, because the one true and satisfying answer is found in the person of Jesus Christ.

Not only are we saved by Jesus' death on a cruel cross, but God has also given us the Holy Spirit, who gives wisdom, opens doors of opportunity, convicts of sin, and brings comfort to those who grieve. **John 16:7-11** says:

> "Nevertheless I tell you the truth. It is to your advantage that I go away; for if I do not go away, the Helper will not come to you; but if I depart, I will send Him to you. And when He has come, He will convict the world of sin, and of righteousness, and of judgment; of sin, because they do not believe in Me; of righteousness, because I go to My Father and you see Me no more; of judgment because the ruler of this world is judged."

And not only do we have the Holy Spirit living inside us to help us, but the names of God demonstrate that He is the answer to absolutely everything we need—every problem we could ever face. He is Jehovah Jireh, our Provider, (we might even say "our Provision.") He is Jehovah Shalom, our Peace. He is Jehovah Rapha, our Healer, Jehovah Nissi, our Banner, as we go into any battle. He is Jehovah Rohi, our Shepherd, and Jehovah Tsidkenu, our Righteousness. He is Jehovah Mephaulti, our Deliverer, Jehovah Emeth, God of our salvation, Elohe Mauzi, our Strength, Elohim Ozer Li, God our Helper, El Sali, our Rock, El Shaddai, God Almighty or the all-breasted One, (one who nourishes, supplies and satisfies) and Jehovah Machsi, our Refuge, among others. So why aren't we shouting from the rooftops that Jesus is the answer to every question? We have the answer!

1.7 Political Correctness

One of the major reasons for the unpopularity of evangelism is that, in recent years, particularly in the UK and the USA, it has become increasingly politically incorrect to make mention of the name of Jesus or even to wear any form of religious symbols in schools and colleges and places of employment. etc. For example, in 2006 an employee at British Airways was forbidden from wearing her cross visibly on her uniform. In 2009, a nurse was suspended by her North Summerset Primary Care Trust in the UK for offering to pray with a patient. Also in 2009, a primary school receptionist was reprimanded for emailing a request for prayer for her five-year-old daughter who was sharing her faith at school. It is obvious that these high profile cases have produced a culture of fear for those of us wanting to open up a conversation about Jesus, at work, school or with our neighbors.

A couple of years ago I attended a Christmas concert for children at a junior school in the United States. I was horrified to learn that no mention could be made of Jesus, the first Noel etc. or anything relating to Christianity. This is the United States we are talking about here, absurd, don't you think?

1.8 Don't Know How to Witness

Did you know that most believers have no idea how to talk to anyone about Christ? They have no clue how to begin a conversation, and are unaware that the Holy Spirit is with them to help them.

And for those who have been able to lead others to Christ, discouragement can set in because very often, they have not been able to get new converts to be fully transformed, that is, to move from the outer court into the holy of holies. The purpose of salvation is not merely to steer them away from the edge of hell, but to help them put Jesus first, to find their God-given destiny to live with passion and to win souls, completely sold out to the cause of Christ. Our goal then must be to lead others into the fullness of God through meaningful and committed relationship with Christ and nothing less.

Finally and probably most importantly, there are those who simply don't believe they have the necessary interpersonal skills to enable them to share the gospel with others.

Whatever the reason, it is indeed a tragedy that so many, including those who've been saved for years, have not been sharing their faith. I would venture to guess that, if I asked how many have led someone to Christ in the last ten years, the answer would be shocking. Many would have to hang their heads in shame.

If you identify with one of these categories, don't despair, because you are not alone. But do keep reading, because I want to equip you to share the gospel in power, confidence, and love, as never before.

Chapter Checklist

In review:

- Most believers are of the opinion that evangelism is the responsibility of those with special gifts, titles and callings.
- Lack of awareness that witnessing is a Christian duty for every believer.
- Feelings of unworthiness and/or guilt.
- Ashamed to be identified with Christ.
- Lack of preparation.
- Lack of conviction.
- Many simply do not know how to witness.

------------------------------ Questions: ----------------------------------

1. Witnessing is to be left to people with special gifts, talents and titles. True/False

2. Why Has God put you in your place of employment /school right now?

3. What percentage of believers do not constantly witness for Christ?
   95%
   80%
   2%

4. What percentage of believers have never won a single soul for Christ?
   95%
   80%
   2%

5. Name 5 reasons given in this chapter for the lack of enthusiasm.

6. You should not have to tell anyone about God, because they should see it in your life. True/False

7. What scripture cited in this chapter states that we must speak to others about their need for salvation?

8. What is the main reason for the feeling of unworthiness that prevents most Christians from witnessing?

9. How does the enemy use the past to hinder believers from witnessing?

10. How can your past be used as an effective witnessing tool?

11. What was the urgent call that Jesus made in John 4:35?

12. What percentage of American Churches is growing in real terms?

13. Why is God crowded out of a central place in human thoughts and values?

____

14. The world is desperate for the gospel. True/False

____

Personal Notes

____

____

____

____

____

____

____

____

____

____

____

____

____

____

= CHAPTER TWO =

Knowing You are Called to be a Witness

What do you think is the number one reason for the lack of personal evangelism in the local church? Clearly, because we aren't all convinced that hell equals eternal doom, we fail to be alarmed about the idea of death. If we were actually certain that death is final with no further chance to change one's mind, and that hell is a terrible, God-forsaken place to spend eternity in torture, we would warn everyone we know about their need for a personal Savior.

Even for those who know it's true, witnessing is the most feared, most unpopular ministry in any local church. The question here then is, why? I believe it's because of the lack of awareness. Most are unaware that witnessing is the duty of every believer; and as mentioned earlier, many do not even believe they are called for that purpose, and this is what we are going to discuss in the following paragraphs.

2.1 Understanding the Call

When I ask people if they are aware of the call of God on their lives, they usually give a confused look and a vague answer. They usually say, "I'm not sure," or "I don't know." The truth is that many believers are unsure of the reason they're here. Well, let me make something clear. We are not here merely to take up space until we die. We must be about our Father's business—of reflecting the love of Christ and sharing the good news of salvation. In that regard we must understand the two types of calls upon our lives: the specific call and the general call.

2.1.1 The Specific Call

A specific call is one that is unique to you as an individual and takes into account your special gifts and talents. It is often identified by a natural propensity to perform a certain task with ease and great joy, as if it is a part of your DNA. This kind of call is very individual and cannot be duplicated by anyone else. Each of us has gifts and talents of our own and, though we can learn from others, this is where your natural gift will allow you to develop your own "voice" so you can reach people in ways no one else can.

If you aren't sure of your call there are several things you can do: First of all, you can pray, asking God for wisdom, revelation, and open doors. Habakkuk 2:1 says, "'I will stand my watch and set myself on the rampart, and watch to see what He will say to me and what I will answer.' Then the Lord answered me and said, 'Write the vision, and make it plain on tablets, that he may run who reads it.'"

Note that Habakkuk said the first priority is to set himself on the rampart which is to set himself into a place of prayer, and then to be silent and listen to hear the voice of the Lord. Too often we go to God in prayer with our shopping list but do not bother to stop and listen to hear what God is saying to us. Prayer is a conversation with God and therefore if we are talking to Him we must also expect Him to speak to us. In his case, Habakkuk called out, asking God to address his questions concerning the injustice, violence and

> Habakkuk called out asking God to address his questions concerning the injustice, the violence and the perversion of his nation. We too are to be burdened for the souls of men.

perversion of his people, the tribe of Judah. The Hebrew meaning for "Judah" is praise, therefore these were the people of praise, but note that they were not giving praise to God, in fact they had become rebellious. He felt frustrated, unable to understand why God, who was a God of justice, seemed to take no interest in dealing with the rebellion of the people. That sounds much like us today, doesn't it? We want answers, and we want them now. Perhaps you are wondering why God hasn't yet saved a friend or family member you've been praying for, for years. Somehow Habakkuk seemed to sense that he could only earn the right to speak and get answers if he waited in silence for God to speak.

Notice that Habakkuk wasn't making an unreasonable request. In fact, God tells us to make our requests known to Him, but then He wants us to wait patiently for His answers. Note that at the very moment Habakkuk decided to get into the secret place of prayer with God and listen, he heard the voice of God. God spoke to him, and said this, "Write the vision and make it plan, for the vision is yet for an appointed time, but at the end it will speak, and it will not lie. Though it tarries, wait for it, because it will surely come, it will not tarry."

Whatever you're asking God to do will come to pass in His time if it's according to God's will. And in the meantime, as you wait for your answer, you can get on with the general call.

2.1.2 The General Call

The general call is a call that applies to every believer in the body of Christ. For example, we are all, without exception, called to live a life of holiness. And just as holiness is a general call, so is the call to share the message of the gospel. No one is exempt, and as I said before you need not have a special anointing or title. Nor do you need an education or a degree to be obedient and win the lost.

If you have mistakenly believed that witnessing should be left to those with a special calling, you may have excused yourself and walked away from your responsibility. But if that's the case, you need to re-think that notion. It has been said that each of us has a circle of 250 people we influence, some close and some further away, but because we may be the only Bible they will ever read, it's up to us to share the truth of the gospel with them, or it may never get done. Make no mistake about it: their blood will be required at our hands. Ezekiel 33:8 tells us: "When I say to the wicked, 'O wicked man, you shall surely die!' and you do not speak to warn the wicked from his way, that wicked man shall die in his iniquity; but his blood shall I require at your hand."

Please understand me on this. I am not saying that some are not especially gifted or called in this area, because some are, but that does not excuse the rest of us from winning the souls in our circle. You may not consider yourself to be gifted or indeed to have the required knowledge. When it comes to knowledge, however, you are responsible to feed daily upon God's Word, equipping yourself to know and understand what you have. **Matthew 4:4 say**, "For man shall not live by bread alone but by every word that proceeds from the mouth of God." "You need the sincere meat of the word to grow thereby." Without the daily nourishment of the Word we fail to grow spiritually and can actually stray from the narrow way as our enemy the devil steals the good seed and causes confusion and unbelief to set in. If you aren't completely convinced and passionate about the salvation message you will, in time, find it too difficult to keep the faith and you will walk away.

So what I'm saying then is that, although we require knowledge that is not our only goal. In his letter to Timothy, Paul encourages him to remind the church, "charging them before the Lord, not to strive about words to no profit, to the ruin of the hearers." He then went on to say, "Be diligent to present yourself approved to God, a worker who does not need to be ashamed, rightly dividing the word of truth." Notice that Paul instructed Timothy not to strive with anyone about who has more knowledge. In other words, head knowledge is not what is required to be a witness for Christ. It was in this same context that Paul wrote to the church in **1 Corinthians 2:1-5,**

> "And I, brethren, when I came to you, did not come with excellence of speech or of wisdom declaring to you the testimony of God. For I determined not to know anything among you except Jesus Christ and Him crucified. I was with you in weakness, in fear, and in much trembling. And my speech and my preaching *were* not with persuasive words of human wisdom, but in demonstration of the Spirit and of power, that your faith should not be in the wisdom of men but in the power of God."

Notice that verse 4 says his speech and preaching were not with persuasive words of human wisdom, but rather, in demonstration of the spirit of power. While knowledge is important, it is even more vital that we allow the Holy Spirit to move through us in power, because without a move of the spirit, the process is an exercise of the flesh, and futile. In reality the kingdom of heaven is not in word but in power. The Holy Spirit moving through us is what actually qualifies us to be witnesses for Christ.

2.2 It Is Your Duty as a Disciple of Christ

Once we realize our responsibility to win the lost it is vital to know and understand our role.

If you were asked to act in a movie, your first question would probably be, "What role am I going to play?" The same would be true if you were applying for a job—you would want to know the job description.

The same is also true of the call of God. Knowing He has called you means He has called you out of something and into something else. In this case He's called you out of darkness and into His marvelous light so you can share the truth with those who are desperate to hear.

Once again, I believe this is what **Hosea 4:6** is saying, "My people are destroyed for lack of knowledge." (Knowledge here refers to the awareness of your identity as a witness as opposed to what you need to know to be a witness.) It goes on to say: "Because you have rejected knowledge, I also will reject you from being a priest for Me." Have you noticed that many in the body of Christ are happy to be identified with the kingship of God, but not with their duty as prophets and priests who are to minister to the world on God's behalf? Rejecting our assignment as witnesses actually disqualifies us from our priestly duties. For that reason we should know and accept our duties as prophets, priests and kings, as well as witnesses to the amazing salvation message.

Chapter Checklist

In review:

- As a believer God has a call upon your life to be a witness for Him,
- Witnessing is not as daunting as it appears. There's nothing to be afraid of.
- You must understand the difference between the general and the specific calls of God on your life.
- The specific call involves a direct call from God to do a specific task that lines up with your particular gifts and talents.
- The general call is directed toward every Christian and involves both the call to holiness and the call to win the lost. These calls do not require human acknowledgement or affirmation, because we have been commissioned by heaven.
- Witnessing is your God-ordained duty. Therefore, you are to do what God has called you to do with all your heart, all your soul, all your mind, and all your strength.

------------------------------ Questions: ------------------------------

1. Name two types of calls mentioned in this chapter.

2. Name two reasons why witnessing is the most feared ministry in the body of Christ.

3. What is a specific call?

4. What is a general call?

5. What are the main reasons why witnessing is unpopular among believers?

6. What can you do to help you understand a specific call?

7. What is the fundamental lesson taught by Habakkuk?

---

8. What immediately happened when Habakkuk chose to listen?

---

9. What did God say to Habakkuk?

---

10. What is a good example of a general call?

---

11. What was Paul's advice to Timothy concerning the use of words?

---

12. How did Paul speak to the Corinthians?

---

13. "And I brethren, when I came to you came not with the excellence of speech, declaring to you the testimony of God." What does this verse mean?

---

14. What will happen if we reject the knowledge of God?

Personal Notes

= CHAPTER THREE =

Knowing Your Identity as a Witness for Christ

3.1 Ambassadors for Christ

Did you know that there is a serious identity crisis in the body of Christ? It's true. Most of us do not know who we really are and to whom we belong. And while the vast majority of people are aware of the need to know their identity, they inadvertently go about finding it the wrong way.

For example, many of us think about our identity in Christendom from a positional perspective—with the exception of clergy driven churches—these are churches where the leader does practically everything with the help of a few assistants. The others lived and died without ever realizing their full potential. Otherwise we think that having a position in our local church establishes our identity in the kingdom of God. It is for that reason we often aspire to become ministers, elders, secretaries, teachers, etc. Because to most those positions hold such great importance some might even throw tantrums, disrupt the program or leave the church with an attitude if the leadership refuses to give them positions they desire. The reason for such reactions is that, such actions threaten their self-image. If such things are what defines us we will feel worth less if the position is withheld.

It is for this reason people prefer to be called by their titles and introduce themselves as such rather than simply using their given names. That's why people are often called, "Apostle So-and-So", or "Prophet So-and-So." They are exalted by titles while often hiding their true identities. The thing is, our professions and positions do not make us who we are. We are who we are behind our masks. In fact, a few years ago a well-known and apparently caring family doctor in the UK was found to be a mass murderer, who had been killing his patients for decades before the truth was finally discovered. Though he was known as "Doc," his true identity was that of a murderer.

The thing is, Jesus is to be our model regarding our identity. He, who was actually God, did not flaunt His deity or lord it over anyone—ever. In fact, He left His throne in heaven and became a servant, so that you and I could be exalted. Translated, that means that you and I should also be known as servants, because that is what pleases God. And a servant who is worthy of praise is one who loves others and has their best interests at heart. Someone who has a servant's heart will risk rejection to speak the truth in love regarding the need for a Savior, in order to save someone from eternity in hell.

Once again, your title is not your true identity; your true identity is who you really are behind the façade. According to Scripture you are a witness, an ambassador for Christ. For those who are especially driven by titles, they don't get any better than this one. And what's even better—this one doesn't need the approval of any earthly authority; you've already been commissioned by God and no one can overturn it or take it away. The only one who can render it powerless is you—that is, if you fail to operate according to your true identity as an ambassador for Christ.

Who then is an ambassador? An ambassador is an appointed official or servant messenger. He or she is a diplomatic representative sent by a monarch or state, from one mission to another. An ambassador is a high-ranking diplomat whose main

> We are diplomatic representatives of a government, and probably more importantly, a kingdom. The only difference here is the kingdom is not of this world.

duty is to represent the views of his or her government. In reality, this is who we are. We are diplomatic representatives of a government, a kingdom. The only difference is that, that kingdom is not of this world; it is the heavenly kingdom. Therefore, that makes you a diplomatic official of the Most High God, and in effect, an ambassador of the highest ranking.

3.2 How an Ambassador Represents His Country

With that in mind it will be necessary to learn what it takes to be an ambassador, and more importantly, to learn what it takes to represent the kingdom of God.

Not only have you been called by God, but you've been especially chosen, handpicked by God Himself before the foundation of the world, to be His ambassador. Can you imagine it—He was thinking of you even before Creation!

Not only did He think of you, but He chose you out of billions of others to actually represent His kingdom here on earth!

That is exactly what Paul was saying in Romans 8:28–30: "And we know that all things work together for good to those who love God, to those who are the called according to *His* purpose. For whom He foreknew, He also predestined *to be* conformed to the image of His Son, that He might be the firstborn among many brethren. Moreover whom He predestined, these He also called; whom He called, these He also justified; and whom He justified, these He also glorified."

Please note that God has predestined to you to be conformed to the image of His Son, which means that you are to represent the kingdom of God in the same way Jesus did. As a carrier of His DNA you should represent Him with diplomacy and great distinction just as an ambassador would represent his country. The good news is that it's not as hard as it sounds.

3.3 The Role of an Ambassador

An ambassador's role is one of diplomacy, that is—maintaining good relations between different countries. As a diplomatic representative of God our purpose is to maintain a good relationship between the heavenly and earthly kingdoms. This world is not our home; we are strangers and pilgrims—sojourners. If you get into trouble in another country you may need your country's ambassador to come to your aid. As an ambassador of Jesus Christ your role is to aid the lost and dying—those who are in danger of facing the judgment and wrath of God.

Such knowledge should encourage you and make you confident regarding your place—your niche in the kingdom. You are no longer just an ordinary person with no purpose, but a vital part of the plan of God for the salvation of mankind. You may find it hard to believe, but it's true—as a child of God you are no longer to live for yourself, according to the flesh, but according to the Spirit and will of God.

In his letter to the Corinthians (**2 Corinthians 5:16–20**), Paul says, "Therefore, from now on, we regard no one according to the flesh." He went on to say,

> "Even though we have known Christ according to the flesh, yet now we know Him thus no longer. Therefore, if anyone is in Christ he is a new creation; old things have passed away; behold all things have become new. Now all things *are* of God, who has reconciled us to Himself through Jesus Christ, and has given us the ministry of reconciliation, that is, that God was in Christ reconciling the world to Himself, not imputing their trespasses to them, and has committed to us the word of reconciliation. Now then, we are ambassadors for Christ, as though God were pleading through us: we implore *you* on Christ's behalf, be reconciled to God. For He made Him who knew no sin *to be* sin for us, that we might become the righteousness of God in Him."

Matthew Henry's commentary explains it like this:

> "The renewed man acts upon new principles, by new rules, with new ends, and in new company. The believer is created anew; his heart is not merely set right, but a new heart is given him. He is the workmanship of God, created in Christ Jesus unto good works. Though the same as a man, he is changed in his character and conduct. These words must and do mean more than an outward reformation."

In essence, no true born-again Christian is known after the flesh.

Note the emphasis Paul placed on the importance of reconciliation with God. Therefore, as God is willing to be reconciled to us, we ought to be reconciled to God. And it is the great end and design of the gospel, that word of reconciliation, to prevail upon sinners to lay aside their enmity against God. Faithful believers are Christ's ambassadors, sent to plead with sinners on peace and reconciliation; they come in God's name, with his entreaties, and act in Christ's stead, doing the very thing he did when he was upon this earth, and what he wills to be done now that he is in heaven. Wonderful condescension! Though God can be no loser by the quarrel, nor gainer by the peace, yet by his ministers he beseeches sinners to lay aside their enmity, and accept of the terms he offers, that they would be reconciled to him, to all his attributes, to all his laws, and to all his providences, to believe in the Mediator, to accept the atonement, and comply with his gospel, in all the parts of it and in the whole design of it. And for our encouragement so to do the apostle subjoins what should be well known and duly considered by us.

3.4 The Characteristics of an Ambassador

Ambassadors are excellent communicators and usually possess great problem-solving skills. They are also known for their pleasant personalities. They are builders of relationships between their own country and other nations. As part of their methodology, they keep their focus on those with whom they are communicating. Probably more importantly, their objective is to get their message across as clearly and tactfully as possible. This is essential because they reflect the character of their country to the world.

Notice that when countries are at war, it is the ambassador's duty to patiently and diplomatically explain his country's point of view. You may also notice that they often do so at the expense of their own interests. Because they are diplomats, that is exactly what they are required to do. And we must use the same approach when witnessing. In fact, from the moment you give your life to Christ, and begin to grow in your relationship with Him, you should focus not just on what you believe but on how you behave—because your actions reflect on Christ, and reveal your true priorities.

3.4.1 Not Arrogant by Nature

Have you noticed how easy it is to become prideful and arrogant when given a position as a trainer or a teacher—especially when the trainee needs to be spoon-fed? When it happens it often hinders us from effectively doing the job. In the same way we must be gentle and compassionate toward those with whom we share the gospel. Remember, patience is a virtue. If they don't grasp the gospel easily we must remember that such things are spiritually discerned, which means we must pray that the Holy Spirit gives them understanding and revelation.

It is not always easy to exercise patience in these situations, but patience must be the companion of an ambassador. Have you ever seen a U.S. ambassador interviewed on television during wartime? Have you noticed how hard they try to reflect composure when it's clear they're unhappy about the situation?

It is easy to lose patience when we believe someone should be catching on faster than they are. In fact, I have to admit a personal struggle in this area. Whenever I train new staff, I do not appreciate answering the same question three times. But when that happens I have to remind myself that each of us learns and processes information in different ways. When trying to share the gospel, especially with those who have little knowledge of Christ, patience is essential. It also helps to determine how much they already know, so you can better address their needs. This kind of approach will help them open up their hearts and make them more receptive to your teaching.

3.5 How Ambassadors Respond to Opposition

An ambassador is characterized by diplomacy; therefore you as an ambassador for Christ are required to be extremely diplomatic. You must adopt a professional approach, especially when dealing with someone who has a tendency to want to drag you into a debate. For instance, you cannot afford to be known as short-tempered or argumentative. Your conversation must be "seasoned with salt," so that people want to listen to you. An ambassador must take the time to get all the required information before responding to disagreement. Getting upset or angry will be counterproductive. It will be far more beneficial to calmly explain the facts and show them there is a better way.

3.5.1 You Should Never Take Personal Offense

If you are going to represent the kingdom of heaven with diplomacy and distinction, you must also possess a forgiving spirit. Let's say you are trying to witness to someone who is unpleasant and unkind. Under no circumstances should you take it as a personal offense. And while I understand that you may not hit it off with everyone, it's essential to avoid bringing reproach to the gospel.

As a Christian you must adopt the attitude of Christ when He hung from the cross. He looked with sadness at the perpetrators and said, "Father, forgive them, for they know not what they do." In fact, Scripture says that we must forgive those who offend us or God will not forgive us. **(See Matthew 6:15.)**

Our own imperfections are often the greatest challenges we must overcome, especially when dealing with other people. But it is possible, in the power of the Holy Spirit, to live above those things as we represent Christ.

The bottom line is that you are a diplomatic representative of the kingdom of God here on earth, and there is no higher office than this. You represent the kingdom of the only true God (Elohim), the Mighty God who can create something out of nothing.

This role is something most Christians take lightly, though there are a few who take it seriously. For example, many years ago a friend who is now a pastor, said he had answered an ad to fill the position of ambassador to the Abidjan Embassy in London. At the time I thought it was a crazy idea, so I asked him what prompted him to do that. He explained, "I am an ambassador for Christ. That is what I see in the Bible." Believe it or not, they scheduled an interview and inquired about his qualifications and education. He responded by opening his Bible and pointing them to **2 Corinthians 5**, mentioned above. He was simply making the point that he takes God's Word literally and seriously. No matter how you feel about this story, the truth is that you are an ambassador for Christ.

I must point out here, though, that when Paul said we are ambassadors for Christ, he was not referring to those who are not committed to their faith. He was specifically referring to himself and Timothy. In other words, not everyone who attends worship services, or gets baptized, or claims to be a Christian, can claim to be an ambassador for Christ. In order to be a true ambassador you must be sold out to the cause of Christ, and put Him first in everything.

Chapter Checklist

In review:

- You need to know your identity as a witness for Christ.
- You are an ambassador for Christ.
- You are not the same person you used to be. You are a new creation and can no longer be known according to the flesh, as Paul said of Christ.

Job Description of an Ambassador

- An ambassador must not be quick to respond to conflict.
- An ambassador must learn to forgive and forget.
- Must represent the kingdom with diplomacy and distinction

Understanding who you are in the kingdom will build your confidence as you take your place as an ambassador for Christ.

------------------------------ Questions --------------------------------

1. To what secular profession is a witness likened in this chapter?

2. Who is an ambassador?

3. You have to be appointed by your local pastor before you can become an ambassador for Christ. True/ False

4. How does an ambassador represent his country?

5. What is the role of an ambassador?

6. What is the believer's role as an ambassador for Christ?

7. When does someone need the help of an ambassador?

---

8. How does the answer to question seven apply to an ambassador for Christ?

---

9. What did Paul say in 2 Corinthians 5:16 – 21 about how we are regarded as Christians?

---

10. Name 5 character qualities of an ambassador.

---

11. How do ambassadors respond to opposition?

Personal Notes

SECTION 2

Becoming an Expert Witness

Chapters 4 - 6

= CHAPTER FOUR =

Understanding the Motive for Witnessing

If you are going to be one of the most outstanding witnesses of this generation capable of leading people to Christ on a regular basis, you first must determine your motive for witnessing. For example, you will have to decide whether your motive is out of obligation to your church organization or out of loving obedience to Christ. Or whether your motive is to force others or gently lead them to the truth.

If you fail to understand the point of witnessing, which is to provide evidence based on personal knowledge/experience of the love of Christ—so others will understand God's incredible love and fall in love with a Savior who paid for their redemption, even great zeal and good intentions will fall short of the goal to win souls. If this is merely one more thing on your "To Do" list, you will never be an effective soul winner. More than anything, it's vital that a witness love his prospect so much that he is eager to share the wonderful gift of salvation, rescuing that soul from eternal hell. In fact, you should love that person so much that you will risk rejection to make your point. Having the right motive for witnessing will give you a head start in becoming a powerful witness for Christ.

4.1 Not with Intent to Indoctrinate or for Religious Reasons

It may surprise you to know that you should not witness for religious reasons. By that I mean that you should not testify merely to push your religious ideas on others. Rather, you should simply want to tell them about Jesus. I'm sure you've seen people argue passionately, pushing their church's teachings on others. The truth is that pushing an ideology is not the same as sharing the simple truth that Jesus saves. Witnessing should never be done for the sake of argument or to win a contest. It is not to become a power struggle where we get the upper hand. The Holy Spirit wants us to share how Jesus died in our place, but He needs no hard-sell salesmanship to convince them of their need for a Savior.

To appreciate this concept you must understand what I mean when I use the word "religion." *Webster's Dictionary* defines religion as "The outward act or form which indicates their recognition of the existence of a God or gods having power over their destiny, to whom obedience, service and honor is due; the feeling expressed of human love, fear or awe of some superhuman or overriding power. An orderly life that others are able to observe produced by prudential motives or by habit; but without seriousness; there can be no religious principle at the bottom, no course of conduct from religious motives."

As you can see, the term "religion" was not originally used in place of the word "godliness" but instead expresses an outward form of inward devotion.

You have probably heard people say that their religious beliefs are personal and not up for discussion. Others argue that they have no use for religious fanatics. To that I can only say, "I agree." Does that surprise you? Well, consider this. Christianity is not a religion; it is a relationship with our Creator. A fanatic will push his church's religious ideologies on you, while as a passionate witness you will simply share the truth of your personal testimony, that Jesus loved you, forgave your sins, and transformed your life forever and can do the same for your friends.

There is no room in this equation for doctrinal arguments, so put such thoughts aside and let the Holy Spirit begin to speak through you how Jesus came to "seek and to save that which was lost" and make all things new.

Religious doctrines and strongly held personal beliefs are indeed, best kept private. Did you know that in Jesus' day the religious people were the biggest problem He had to confront? They simply could not accept a simple gospel, without rules and complicated traditions, and they ultimately became a stumbling block to those desperate to hear the truth. Because they felt threatened by a simple salvation message that put no requirements and no costs on the people, the religious leaders wanted to destroy Him. And in the end, they were the ones who plotted and carried out His death. So, no matter what your denominational affiliation, it's vital to set those ties aside for the purpose of winning souls. In other words, don't waste your time telling others about your church. They don't need mere religious traditions or more rules and regulations; they just need Jesus. The subject of church doctrine is one of the greatest hindrances to reaching people with the simple salvation message. Let's get down to what really matters and make it about Jesus rather than about church.

In the end we must love others the same way God does. We must be passionate about what He is passionate about, so that we open our mouths and share the treasure within us with those who need to hear.

4.2 Not to Impress Others

As an expert witness for Christ it's important that you not seek to impress anyone. Because you represent Christ you must seek the heart of God and adopt the attitude of a servant, who cares more about the soul you want to win than you care about yourself. And while it's important to put your best foot forward, God can work through you, a willing vessel, whether you present yourself perfectly or not. The anointing of God is powerful, and He promises that His Word will not return void.

Paul summed this up beautifully in **1 Corinthians 2:1-5:**

> "And I, brethren, when I came to you, came not with excellence of speech or of wisdom declaring unto you the testimony of God. For I determined not to know anything among you, save Jesus Christ and Him crucified. And I was with you in weakness, and in fear and in much trembling." And note this: "And my speech and my preaching were not with enticing words of man's wisdom, but in demonstration of the spirit and of power, that your faith should not stand in the wisdom of men, but in the power of God."

Then He went on to say,

> "However, we speak wisdom to those who are mature, yet not the wisdom of this age, or of the rulers of this age who are coming to nothing. But we speak the wisdom of God in a mystery, the hidden mystery which God ordained before the ages for our glory, which none of the rulers of this world knew; for had they known, they would not have crucified the Lord of glory. But as it is written, eyes have not seen, nor ears heard, nor have entered into the heart of man the things which God has prepared for those who love Him. But God has revealed them to us through His Spirit. For the spirit searches all things, yes, and the deep things of God. For what man knows the things of a man except the spirit of the man which is in him? Even so no one knows the things of God except the Spirit of God. Now we have not received the spirit of this world, but the Spirit who is from God, that we might know the things

> that have been freely given to us by God. These things we also speak, not in words which man's wisdom teaches but which the Holy Spirit teaches, comparing spiritual things with spiritual. But the natural man does not receive the things of the Spirit of God for they are foolishness to him; nor can he know them for they are spiritually discerned."

In essence he was reminding the Corinthians of the simple, straightforward way he shared the gospel, which was a treasure, as well as wisdom of the highest order. He wanted them to know that such wisdom exceeded the achievements of the most learned men. It was clearly wisdom that only God could impart by the power of the Spirit. And you and I should also share with others sincerely and simply.

The following is a summary of how Paul acted:

- He resolved to *know* nothing among them but Jesus Christ and Him crucified—not theology, not philosophy, not science, and not worldly wisdom.
- He purposed in his heart to *make a show* of no other knowledge than that of Christ.
- He determined to *preach* nothing but Christ and Him crucified.
- He was determined to pursue nothing but Jesus Christ who in His person and offices is the "sum and substance of the gospel." This then ought to be the subject of any preaching or witnessing. This is powerful stuff. And finally;
- He determined not to allow his speech and preaching to be with enticing words of man's wisdom. Paul did not want to exalt himself with a dazzling display of words, or extraordinary theological and philosophical abilities. He did not set himself up to captivate the mind or the ear with eloquent expressions.

Notice also that Paul spoke to them in weakness, fear, and trembling; and yet his preaching clearly demonstrated the power of the Holy Spirit and moved people to repentance. It is also important to note that Paul had enemies right in the church at Corinth who did not always speak well of him. And if they didn't speak well of Paul, they may not speak well of you. But what does it matter? So long as you are doing the will of God it's all right—in the end God's opinion is the only one that counts. Their opinion was that his human presence was weak and his speech pathetic. **(See 2 Corinthians 10:10.)** It is said that Paul was a small man and spoke with a low voice, but though he was not an impressive presence, he spoke with authority and power when under the power of the Holy Spirit.

Paul had little use for the opinions of others—he simply chose to get on with the task at hand no matter what anyone else thought. He was by no means terrified by his adversaries. He represented his office as an ambassador with much modesty, concern, and care. He behaved with great humility among them, and not as one caught up with the honor and authority placed on him, but as one concerned with proving himself faithful to his calling, lest he misrepresent that which God had placed in his trust.

Can you see why this issue is not about us? Did you know that no faithful ambassador of Christ puts confidence in his own natural ability? Whether you believe it or not many preachers experience much fear and trembling despite a godly passion to win souls for the kingdom. They often experience a deep sense of their own weakness, because they know that in and of themselves they are insufficient apart from the Holy Spirit of God. When He moves in power, signs and wonders, they feel humble, knowing they are merely vessels for His use and must give glory to God instead of taking credit for themselves. And when God moves to convict and convince men of their need for salvation, nothing can stand against it.

So why did Paul preach in the way he did? "So that your faith should not stand in the wisdom of man, but the power of God" **(1 Corinthians 2:5)** "That they might not be drawn by human motives, nor overcome by mere human arguments, lest it should be said that either rhetoric or logic had made them Christians. But, when nothing but Christ crucified was plainly preached, the success must be founded, not on human wisdom, but divine evidence and operation. The gospel was so preached that God might appear and be glorified in all."

4.3 We Witness Because of the Importance of the Soul

It is my belief that at one time or another we all have to deal with the question of what happens to the soul after we die. It is a universal question. Since the beginning of time man has sought the answer to the question of what happens to those who have gone on before and whether we will see them again.

It is also every man's desire to know that his life has meaning and purpose, and he is desperate to know whether or not death is the end or merely the beginning of something else.

The most common Christian belief regarding life after death is that people possess souls and at death their consciousness in the form of that soul, departs from the body and heads for heaven or hell.

While some believe that death is the end others choose to believe that if the body is cremated and the ashes scattered, they will not be found and held accountable on the Day of Judgment, though the Bible says otherwise. If you agree with such a belief you are probably saying that man is nothing but a piece of clay, while the truth is that man is made up of three parts—body, soul and spirit. That is why you must not judge a person by his physical appearance; instead you must check out his character. The character of a person is what is referred to as the soul. The soul is made up of the mind, the emotions, and the will. So God breathed into man and he became a living soul; therefore, apart from the soul, man ceases to live.

The concept of life after death is not only a Christian phenomenon. In fact, most world religions teach some form of life after death. For example, the ancient Egyptians practiced complex rituals and ceremonies to usher the pharaohs into eternity.

Massive pyramids and complex mazes of tombs were constructed and filled with items the dead would supposedly need in the afterlife.

In other civilizations, when the ruler died it is said that those who served him during his lifetime were also put to death so they could immediately serve him in the afterlife. Often his servants, his wife, and other relatives, and sometimes even household pets joined him in death.

Even pagan Greek philosophers such as Socrates, Plato, and Aristotle believed in the idea of the immortality of the soul. For example:

Socrates

Socrates' presentation of death says, "Is it not the separation of soul and body? And to be dead is the completion of this; when the soul exists in itself, and is released from the body and body is released from the soul, what is this but death?"

Socrates went on to explain that the immortal soul, once freed from the body, is rewarded according to good deeds or punished for evil. Socrates lived from 470–399 B.C., so his view of the soul actually predated Christianity.

Plato

Plato, who lived 428-348 B.C., argued that man's existence was divided into the material and spiritual, or what he called "ideal" realms. "Plato reasoned that the soul, being eternal, must have had a pre-existence in the ideal world where it learned about the eternal ideals."

Aristotle

"Aristotle argued that the soul does not exist without a body and yet it is not itself a kind of body. For it is not a body, but something which belongs to a body, and for this reason exists in a body"

Here Aristotle was saying that although the soul is not a material thing it is inseparable from the body.

The bottom line is this: Most people believe in the existence of the soul. And since they agree on that issue, the next question is: "How can we determine the final destination of the soul after we die?" The only authoritative answer comes from the Bible, where it addresses the subject in **Ecclesiastes 7:2,** "Death is the destiny of every man and the living should take it to heart." **Hebrews 9:27** goes on to say, "And as it is appointed for men to die once, but after this the judgment, so Christ was offered once to bear the sins of man. To those who eagerly wait for Him He will appear a second time, apart from sin, for salvation."

Here the Bible is saying that it is of paramount importance for people to hear the good news of the gospel of Christ and the need for forgiveness of sin. It is, in fact, a matter of life and death. That should motivate us as believers to ensure that everyone hears the gospel before they die. That is my motivation for witnessing.

From the moment of birth, every man is destined to die one day, but "it is not the will of God that any should perish, but that everyone should come to repentance" **(2 Peter 3:9).** This verse emphasizes how much God treasures the souls of men. In fact, He places such high value on men's souls that He left the splendor of heaven to give His life to redeem us from the jaws of death and hell. **(See Luke 19:10.)**

Jesus' concern for the lost was so deep that it often brought Him to tears. The apostle Paul, too, was so passionate that he literally begged men to be reconciled to God.

Since the time of the early church, God has raised up men and women of vision who are passionate for the souls of men, and we should be no exception. We need to develop a deep passion to win souls for the kingdom of God.

4.4 Because the Message of Salvation is Good News

The problem with most people is that they don't know they are lost. Many struggle to believe that their sin will actually separate them from God for eternity. But most of them are already subconsciously aware that there is something missing and often try to fill the void with other things, to kill the pain of uncertainty. The good news of the gospel has a way of clearing up those doubts for good. As we let them know they have sinned and are separated from God we can also share the truth of God's amazing love, and how He took their place on a cruel cross to snatch them back from the Devil's clutches. What better news can there be than that?

The gospel of Christ is the greatest news that has ever been told in the history of mankind. The word *gospel* actually means "good news" or "glad tidings." In fact, the angel said to the shepherds, "Behold I bring you good tidings of great joy which shall be to all people." It would therefore be a crime for us to keep such an incredible and life-giving revelation to ourselves. In **Luke 8:16,** Jesus said, "No one, when he has lit a lamp, covers it with a vessel or puts it under a bed, but sets it on a lamp stand, that those who enter may see the light."

4.5 To Testify of What They Know about Jesus

When a person is summoned by a court of law to act as a witness, he is actually ordered to give evidence in court concerning that particular case. As it is in the natural, so it is in the spiritual. We have been called as God's witnesses and our duty as witnesses is to give evidence—in this case, to give evidence of Christ. **Isaiah 43:10, tells us:** "You, O Israelites! All you that are called by my name, you are all my witnesses, and so is my servant whom I have chosen."

It was Christ himself that was so described (Ch. 42:1). "All the prophets that testified to Christ, and Christ himself, the great prophet, are here appealed to as God's witnesses. (1.) God's people are witnesses for him, and can attest, upon their own knowledge and experience, concerning the power of his grace, the sweetness of his comforts, the tenderness of his providence, and the truth of his promise. They will go forward to witness for him that he is gracious and that no word of his has fallen to the ground. (2.) His prophets are in a particular manner witnesses for him, with who his secret is, and who know more of him than others do. But the Messiah especially is given to be a witness for him to the people; having lain in his bosom from eternity, he has declared him. Now..."

From an evangelistic perspective, according to Isaiah 43 there are a number of things a witness is called to do.

Witnesses are called to testify of what they know about Jesus. **Isaiah 43:12** says, "I have declared and saved, I have proclaimed and there was no foreign gods among you; therefore you are my witnesses," says the Lord, "that I am God." What is the Scripture saying here? It is saying that we are to be witnesses, but to whom are we to witness? To those who don't yet know that He is the One, true God. Therefore, those of us who acknowledge that the Lord is God should be ready to declare to others what we know of Him. But why are we to do this? We are to do this so that they also may be brought into the knowledge and acknowledgement of who God is. Isaiah did not leave us in ignorance, he went on to give an illustration of who God is.

Isaiah 43: 13-21 tells us:

> Indeed before the day was, I am He; And there is no one who can deliver out of My hand; I work, and who will reverse it?" Thus says the LORD, your Redeemer; The Holy One of Israel: for your sake I will send to Babylon, And bring them all down as fugitives — The Chaldeans, who rejoice in their ships. I am the LORD, your Holy One, The Creator of Israel, your King." Thus says the LORD, who makes a way in the sea and a path through the mighty waters, who brings forth the chariot and horse, the army and the power (They shall lie down together, they shall not rise. They are extinguished, they are quenched like a wick): "Do not remember the former things, Nor consider the things of old. Behold, I will do a new thing; now

it shall spring forth. Shall you not know it? I will even make a road in the wilderness and rivers in the desert. The beast of the field will honor Me, The jackals and the ostriches. Because I give waters in the wilderness and rivers in the desert, go give drink to My people, My chosen. This people I have formed for Myself; they shall declare My praise." We have been chosen to declare the praise of our God Most High.

I believed, therefore have I spoken. Particularly, "Since you cannot but know, and believe, and understand, you must be ready to bear record, That I am he, the only true God that I am a being self-existent and self-sufficient; I am he whom you are to fear, and worship, and trust in. Nay, before the day was (before the first day of time, before the creation of the light, and, consequently, from eternity) I am He. The idols were but of yesterday, new gods that came newly up (**Deut. 32:17**); but the God of Israel was from everlasting. That there was no God formed before me, nor shall be after me. But God has a being from eternity, yea, and a religion in this world before there were either idols or idolaters (truth is more ancient than error); and he will have a being to eternity, and will be worshipped and glorified when idols are famished and abolished and idolatry shall be no more. True religion will keep its ground, and survive all opposition and competition. Great is the truth, and will prevail. That I, even I, am the Lord, the great Jehovah, who is, and was, and is to come; and besides me there is no Savior, v. 11. See what it is that the great God glories in, not so much that he is the only ruler as that he is the only Savior; for

> he delights to do good: he is the Savior of all men" **(1 Timothy 4:10).**

People give all kinds of reasons for rejecting the gospel. You should not be put off by that, however, because it only reveals the sinfulness of man's heart.

Despite their desperation for God's love they reject it because of rebellion and self-will. But whether it seems like it or not, most people, deep inside, are desperate for God despite their attitude in public. I can assure you that should you run into them behind closed doors, especially when they struggle with bereavement or other bad news, many, even from other religions, are quick to call on the name of Jesus. Therefore, under no circumstances should you be afraid to tell the world about Jesus and neither should you feel inadequate. As God said to Jeremiah in Jeremiah Chapter 1, "Before I formed you in the womb I knew you; before you were born I sanctified you; I ordained you a prophet to the nations. Then said I behold I cannot speak, for I am a youth. But the Lord said to me, do not say, I am a youth, for you shall go to all to whom I send you, and whatever I command you, you shall speak."

And please note that it says in **Jeremiah 1:8**: "'Do not be afraid of their faces, for I am with you to deliver you,' says the Lord." Like Jeremiah, you may not see yourself as qualified for the task; you may think you cannot speak and have no idea what to say. But let me assure you that God promises He will be there to assist and deliver you in difficult situations.

Moses had this same problem when God called him to go and deliver the people from Egyptian bondage.

> Then Moses said to the Lord, "O my Lord, I am not eloquent, neither before nor since You have spoken to Your servant; but I am slow of speech and slow of tongue." So the Lord said to him, who has made man's mouth? Or who makes the mute, the deaf, the seeing, or the blind? Have not I, the Lord? "Now therefore go and I will be with

> your mouth and teach you what you shall say." But he said, "O my Lord, please send by the hand of whomsoever else You may send." So the anger of the Lord was kindled against Moses. **Exodus 4: 10 - 14**

Let me put this in perspective for you. Notice that when God called Moses he proceeded to make the excuse that he did not possess the necessary eloquence of speech required for the job. And notice that God responded by saying that it is He who made man's mouth and therefore he must go and that HE will be with his mouth. You see my friends, it is God who made your mouth and therefore when God calls you to go and rescue people from the bondage of their sins He has already equipped you with everything you need for the task. There is nothing to fear. Yes, you may feel inadequate but it is the spirit of God that is working in you both to will and to do His good pleasure.

4.6 We Witness Because Jesus Commanded Us to

The final reason for witnessing is that Jesus commanded it. This is what biblical scholars referred to in Matthew 28 as the Great Commission. "Go you therefore and make disciples of all nations." This passage provides every individual in the body of Christ with a "blueprint" concerning our responsibility as witnesses, which should not be taken lightly. This is more than a proposal; it's a command, which means: to order or compel; it also means to dominate, or to have dominion. We are to take dominion over God's created order.

Chapter Checklist

In review

- It is vital to be aware of your objective in witnessing: to share the love of Jesus rather than to promote a particular church's agenda.

- It is not a platform from which to argue doctrinal issues or prove how much you know. Arguing is addressed specifically in **2 Corinthians 10:4-5:**
- "For though we walk in the flesh we do not war according to the flesh, for the weapons of our warfare are not carnal but mighty in God for the pulling down of strongholds, casting down arguments and every high thing that exalts itself against the knowledge of God." Our sole motive then is to tell the world about Christ and His death on the cross for the salvation of mankind.
- The objective is not to indoctrinate.
- We are to witness because of the importance of saving men's souls from destruction.
- We witness because the news of salvation is good news, which is what the word "gospel" actually means.
- We witness to testify of what we know about Jesus. And finally;
- We witness because we are commanded by Christ to do so.

---------------------------------- Questions ----------------------------------

1. What are the objectives of a witness?

2. What important criteria should be used when dealing with those who are immature?

3. Name at least 3 ways Paul acted when he preached to the Corinthians.

4. Name 3 reasons why we witness.

5. One of the motives for witnessing is to indoctrinate. True/ False

6. The teaching of your church organization is more important than helping someone come to Christ. True or False

7. Being religious is the same as being godly. True/False

---

8. Devil worship is a religion. True or False

---

9. Every true ambassador has full confidence in his own ability. True/False

---

10. The gospel of Christ must be preached with simplicity and clarity. True/False

---

11. Why did Paul purpose in his heart to preach nothing but Christ and Him crucified?

---

12. The concept of life after death is strictly a Christian philosophy. True/False

---

Personal Notes

= CHAPTER FIVE =

Understanding How to Witness

Now, this is where we get down to the nuts and bolts of witnessing. In the previous chapters we've discussed the **reason** why we should witness—the importance of knowing we are **called** to be witnesses—the need to know and understand our **identity** as a witness for Christ—and the importance of understanding our **motive** for witnessing. In this section we will look at how to master the art of personal evangelism from a practical perspective. I will help you discover why you can and should witness like experts, the spirit in which witness should be conducted, and what help you have at your disposal to get the job done fearlessly and successfully.

5.1 Like Experts

Ordinary people just like you can witness like experts. Did you know that? It's true. But there are specific requirements that must be met to be considered an expert. Let's look at them in detail.

To be qualified as an expert you must be knowledgeable and well-versed on your subject. Wikipedia, the online encyclopedia, describes an expert as "someone widely recognized as a reliable source of technique or skill whose faculty for judging or deciding rightly, justly, or wisely is accorded authority and status by their peers or the public in a specific, well-distinguished domain." Generally, an expert is someone with extensive knowledge or ability based on research, experience, or occupation in a particular area of study. An expert can be, by virtue of credentials, training, education, profession, publication, or experience, believed to have special knowledge of a subject beyond that of the average person, sufficient that others may officially (and legally) rely upon that individual's opinion. Historically, an expert was also referred to as a sage (a wise person). The individual was usually a profound thinker distinguished for wisdom and sound judgment. Experts have a history of prolonged or intense experience through practice and education in a particular field. In specific fields, the definition of expert is well established by consensus, and therefore it is not necessary for an individual to have professional or academic qualifications to be accepted as an expert. In this respect, farmers with fifty years of experience sowing seeds and tending flocks would be widely recognized as having complete expertise in the use of times and seasons for sowing and reaping, and the care of animals.

An expert with his vast store of knowledge is able to be flexible in his testimony, gearing it specifically to suit his audience. In the same way, as witnesses of the gospel you and I can pray, asking for discernment to know how to address the specific, felt needs of our audience. Remember God is not necessarily looking for the academically qualified or the naturally skilful or gifted—He's looking for the available. If you then will avail yourself to the service of the Lord, God will use you like an expert.

5.2 It should only be done with a Servant's Heart

Perhaps, no other scripture highlights this point as well as Philippians 2:3-11

> "'Let nothing be done through self ambition or conceit, but in the lowliness of mind let each esteem others better than himself. Let each of you look out not only for his own interest, but also for the interest of others. Let this mind

> be in you which was also in Christ Jesus, who being in the form of God, did not consider it robbery to be equal with God, but made himself of no reputation, taking the form of a bond servant, and coming in the likeness of men. And being found in appearance as a man, He humbled Himself and became obedient to the point of death, even the death of the cross. Therefore God also highly exalted Him and given Him the name which is above every name, that at the name of Jesus every knee should bow, of those in heaven, and of those on earth, and that every tongue should confess that Jesus Christ is Lord, to the glory of God the father.'"

Clearly, we are servant witnesses chosen by God, so it is of paramount importance that we represent the kingdom with the attitude of a servant. The Bible instructs us to serve one another, and an attitude of **servanthood** simplifies that process. For instance, if you see yourself as a servant rather than feeling as if you must perform, the pressure dissipates so that you can be yourself instead of something you're not.

As representatives of Jesus Christ there should be no room in our witness for a judgmental spirit. When presenting Christ to the world we must do so with love and a gentle spirit. No matter what the situation we should act with compassion and understanding. After all, we are all only sinners saved by grace, and none of us is better or more deserving than others. **Ephesians 2:8-9** confirms this when it says: "For by grace you have been saved through faith; and that not of yourselves; it is the gift of God, not of works lest many man should boast." In other words, it is only because of His grace and mercy that He brought us out of darkness and into His marvelous light, for which we should be sincerely grateful.

As we allow the Holy Spirit to flow through us, the beauty of Jesus can be seen in us in all His passion and purity. Perhaps for the very first time an unbeliever can see Jesus through our actions as we share the gospel in a warm and uncomplicated way, painting a word picture of His amazing love. Hearts will be touched when they learn how He who was perfect, gave up His glory to go to a cruel cross, to pay for our salvation.

5.3 You Have Divine Help

It should be comforting to know that you don't have to prove yourself because you will never have to witness alone. Because He was well aware of the magnitude and the complexity of the challenge, Jesus not only commanded us to share the gospel, but He also promised that the Holy Spirit would come and assist us with the task of witnessing, even down to the very words we speak.

Even from Old Testament times God has promised His divine presence would go with His people.

> **In Joshua 1:1-9** we read: "After the death of Moses the servant of the LORD, it came to pass that the LORD spoke to Joshua the son of Nun, Moses' assistant, saying: 'Moses My servant is dead. Now therefore, arise, go over this Jordan, you and all these people, to the land which I am giving to them—the children of Israel. Every place that the sole of your foot will tread upon I have given you, as I said to Moses. From the wilderness and this Lebanon as far as the great river, the River Euphrates, all the land of the Hittites, and to the Great Sea toward the going down of the sun, shall be your territory. No man shall be able to stand before you all the days of your life; as I was with Moses, so I will be with you. I will not leave you nor forsake you. Be strong and of good courage, for to this people you shall divide as an inheritance the land which I swore to their fathers to give them. Only be strong and

> very courageous, that you may observe to do according to all the law which Moses My servant commanded you; do not turn from it to the right hand or to the left, that you may prosper wherever you go. This Book of the Law shall not depart from your mouth, but you shall meditate in it day and night, that you may observe to do according to all that is written in it. For then you will make your way prosperous, and then you will have good success. Have I not commanded you? Be strong and of good courage; do not be afraid, nor be dismayed, for the LORD your God is with you wherever you go.'"

You may say you can't do it, but God says, you "can do all things through Christ who strengthens you." And if you say it is impossible, the Bible says, "All things are possible" (**Luke 18:27**).

As it was in the Old Testament, so it is in the new because Jesus also left us a promise of the Holy Spirit.

> "And being assembled together with them, He commanded them not to depart from Jerusalem, but to wait for the promise of the Father, which, He said, you have heard from me; For John truly baptized with water, but you shall be baptized with the Holy Spirit not many days from now. Therefore, when they had come together, they asked Him saying, Lord, will you at this time restore the kingdom to Israel? And He said to them, "It is not for you to know times or seasons which the Father has put in His own authority. But you shall receive power when the Holy Spirit has come upon you and you shall be witnesses to me, in Jerusalem, and in all Judea and Samaria, and to the end of the earth" **(Acts 1: 4–8).**

The 21st century church faces the same problem today, as many believers are waiting for a certain season of anointing to arrive to encourage them to preach the gospel with power. But the time for waiting is past. The fields are white unto harvest, and the Holy Spirit is already here, waiting on us to step out in faith and speak, for at that point He will fill our mouths with anointed words as we simply move in obedience.

Notice that Jesus was speaking His final words to His disciples before leaving earth. When they asked Jesus when His kingdom would come, Jesus did not tell them, but instead He imparted knowledge to them regarding a vision about reaching the world with the gospel. Note what He told them. He told them to "stay in Jerusalem."

Why were they to stay in Jerusalem? They were to stay there until they received power. Why was it necessary to receive this power? One of the main reasons was because, the task of evangelism would have been impossible without the "exousia" power of the Holy Spirit. And because it would arrive in God's timing, it was necessary to wait until it came, which also meant some who weren't willing to wait, actually missed out when the power finally fell. So the question then followed: "Have you received power since you believed?" It's important to note that the power could not be conjured up by human flesh, but was only available through a move of the Holy Spirit. In other words, He was saying that *after the wait* "the Holy Spirit will come upon you and you shall be witnesses unto me both in Jerusalem and in all Judea."

How then do we receive such power? By hungering after it, God gives it to those who desperately seek it. And where does that hunger come from? It comes from the Holy Spirit who places inside us the desires of the heart of God. And when we hunger after the power, He will motivate us to speak with a passion about the marvelous goodness of God.

Note that following the wait in Jerusalem and the receiving of power, they were to move into all Judea—a neighboring community.

For those of you who have waited in your Jerusalem and received power, assuming that you have shared the gospel with your families, neighbors, and friends, it is high time that you move out into the neighboring communities. Or perhaps you are someone who has not yet laid upon your face to wait before God, which could also mean you have not yet received power. Don't panic—it is not as difficult as you think. God has made a promise, and that promise is yes and amen. All that is required of you is that you are fully surrendered to God. **Matthew 5:6** said, "Blessed are those who hunger and thirst for righteousness, for they ***shall*** be filled." Note the word "shall"—no ifs or buts or maybes. You shall be filled.

Once you have taken care of business at home—that is, your Jerusalem—you will be ready to take the message of salvation to nearby communities. But don't stop there. From there you are to go farther, taking the message to the world.

Maybe you ought to wait in your closet. If you do not have a closet, use your room. Close your door, and "The Father who sees in secret will reward you openly." Maybe your Jerusalem is your town and that may be a small, humble area, but no area should be too small, because each person is important. In fact, although Jesus had very large crusades He was all about seeking out individuals and dealing with them one on one, and because He is our model, we should follow His example. I say this because often people want to skip the ministry to their small local areas and take a giant leap to fancy platforms under bright spotlights, before television cameras, or in massive crusades.

It's important to note that it's not our job to change anyone; rather the Holy Spirit is responsible for saving souls and adding them to the kingdom.

According to Acts Chapter 1, Jesus showed Himself to several people, providing "infallible proof" that He was alive. And no matter what anyone else believes, Christianity is the only ideology that teaches we serve a living God. Jesus is alive, hallelujah!

It was during that period that He gave the Great Commission to the church. Matthew 28:19 says: "And Jesus came and spoke to them saying, 'All authority has been given to Me in heaven and on earth. Go therefore and make disciples from all nations, tribes, and tongues, baptizing them in the name of the Father, and the name of the Son, and the name of the Holy Spirit, teaching them to observe all things that I have commanded you, and lo, I am with you always, even to the end of the age, amen.'" With that promise you can rest assured that whenever you witness for Christ, His presence goes with you.

From this scripture passage it's clear that spreading the gospel is the job of every believer. And that doesn't mean we occasionally set aside a week for evangelistic meetings in our home churches, hoping unbelievers will come in and be saved. Our churches should already be evangelized, so there is little need to cover the same ground again and again with those who are saved. What our churches need—what our hearts need is revival—we need a mighty move of the spirit to set us on fire so that we move out of our comfort zones through the front doors of our churches, and passionately take to the streets where the needs are.

Chapter Checklist

In review:

- Regardless of your background or ability you can witness with meekness and love in the power of the Holy Spirit.
- Though we should do everything with excellence and be as well-prepared as possible, that doesn't mean we have to have a degree on the subject to become an expert.
- We are never alone when witnessing, because Jesus promised the Holy Spirit would be our constant companions equipping us for every good work.
- Because God's answers are always "Yea and amen" to the requests of those who seek Him with all their hearts, souls and minds, He will empower us when we fall in love with Him, hungry for the power and boldness to win souls, for this is His greatest desire.
- Irrespective of our individual abilities and backgrounds, we are guaranteed to be able to witness like an expert provided we do so with a spirit of meekness and love.

- An expert is a person with extensive knowledge based on research but it is also based on prolonged, intense experience through practice. In other words, we don't need academic qualification to be classified as experts.
- We are never alone when witnessing because we will always have the presence of the Holy Spirit with us.
- Hunger for the things of God will empower us and give us boldness to witness.

------------------------------- Questions: -------------------------------

1. How does a person become classified as an expert?
2. Is it necessary for an expert to have professional or academic qualifications? True/False
3. In what spirit should we witness?
4. In what spirit should we not witness?
5. Why is it important to witness in love and compassion?
6. According to Matthew 28:19-20 Jesus left us a command and a promise. What was the command?
7. What was that promise?

8. Why did Jesus tell the disciples to go and wait for the Holy Spirit to come?

Personal Notes

= CHAPTER SIX =

How to Prepare Yourself to Witness

Make no mistake about it, it will take preparation and planning to make a lasting impact on the world when it comes to the salvation of souls. In other words you will have to be proactive about it, for example;

6.1 You Have to Want to Do It

I cannot overemphasize this strongly enough: If you are to be effective at winning souls, not only will you need to want it desperately, you must prepare your heart and mind, setting aside your own agenda, exchanging them for something new—a vision for souls.

As was mentioned earlier it's impossible to sell something you don't believe in, which is why you need to fan the flames of your faith, meditating on what Jesus has done for you. From that point you need to ask God to give you His heart for the lost, seeing what He sees, with the urgency He feels. Without that you won't see the need to share the gospel. On the other hand, once you feel that sense of urgency no one will be able to stop you from warning the lost about hell.

This is pretty much the same as trying to get backers for a new invention. If you are to succeed, you must convince manufacturers to take on your project. You yourself must not only be convinced but you must be consumed by an urgent desire to make it happen.

A couple of years ago, I was witnessing to a young English fellow in my local gym, and he politely informed me that he had everything he needed and had no need for God. Why do you suppose he felt that way? He explained that his uncle was a minister in a local church, but admitted that even his uncle "did not take it seriously." His uncle basically lived his life like anybody else with no particular pressing need for God. You see, because the uncle was not consumed with passion for the things of God he could not convince his nephew.

Many of you have seen little or no growth in your church for many years. There have been no new converts and hopes are dim that, that will change in the foreseeable future. In some cases the church anticipated that the children would grow up, give their lives to the Lord and assume the leadership, while the children, who saw nothing worth having, couldn't wait to jump ship as soon as possible. If that describes your situation I want to offer hope to you, because you can be the catalyst that will turn the situation around once you grasp the vision for souls, know how to win them.

6.2 You Must Be a Student of God's Word

God's Word is the foundation of the gospel and without it we have nothing to offer the unbeliever.

At this point you may argue that in Chapter three that I said a degree or a great store of knowledge wasn't essential. To clear up any confusion let me say it this way: It's not what you know in your head; it's what is in your heart. **Deuteronomy 30:11-14** tells us: "For this commandment which I command you today, it is not too mysterious for you, nor is it far off. It is not in heaven, that you should say, 'Who will ascend into heaven for us and bring it to us, that we may hear and do it?' Nor is it beyond the sea, that you should say, 'Who will go over the sea and bring it to us, that we may hear and do it?' But the word is very near you, in your mouth and in your heart, that you may do it." And if it's indeed true that the Word of God is in us, we will naturally speak at the appropriate time if we are walking in the spirit. "The mouth of the righteous speaks wisdom, and his tongue talks of justice. The law of his God is in his heart" (**Psalm 37:30-31**). Therefore, if you are going to create and leave a lasting impression on the lives of the people to whom you are witnessing, your presentation of Christ to the world has to be rooted in the Word of God.

"Your word I have hidden in my heart, that I might not sin against You" (**Psalm 119:11**).

A reminder: Once the opportunity arises for us to witness we must not waste it to express personal opinions or get into doctrinal arguments. Rather it's time to proclaim that Jesus is the only way to heaven.

I once read the story of a man whose wife worked two jobs to support their family so he could study the Scriptures in order to debate with other Christians at his local café. He did it as a hobby, but from God's perspective it was a total waste of time. Notice the admonition of the apostle Peter in **1 Peter 2:11–12:** "Beloved, I beg *you* as sojourners and pilgrims, abstain from fleshly lusts which war against the soul, having your conduct honorable among the Gentiles, that when they speak against you as evildoers, they may, by *your* good works which they observe, glorify God in the day of visitation."

We are called to present the Word of God so that the power of God will bring a revelation of the need for salvation. **Hebrew 4:12** says, "For the word of God is living and powerful, and sharper than any two edge sword, piercing to the division of the soul and spirit, and of joints and morrow, and it is the discerner of the thoughts and intent of the heart." My friends, the Word of God is a powerful living thing that convicts of sin and brings hearts to repentance.

The Greek word for soul is *psuche*, which describes the part of us that makes us human. This is the mind, the emotions, and the will. Let me tell you what the writer of Hebrews is saying here, and why it is important in this context. As you know, we as human beings are made up of body, soul, and spirit. But there is a problem—we have a natural tendency to gravitate toward the things of the flesh, i.e., the natural stuff as opposed to the things of the spirit. That was what David was talking about in **Psalm 119:25** when he said "My soul is clinging to the dust." This means that our minds, our emotions and our will tend to cling to the natural. But thanks to God this is not the conclusion of the matter, and that's what **Hebrews 4:12** is saying concerning the sharpness and the power of the Word to the dividing of the *psuche* (soul) ***from*** the flesh. Therefore, despite the fact that the soul has a natural propensity to cling to the flesh, the Word of God is far more powerful to bring about separation of both. This is why you must use the Word of God and let it do its work.

And remember; don't let yourself be tempted to flaunt your knowledge of Scripture. Rather, stay focused on sharing the Word with the right heart and the right motive.

6.3 You Must Be Willing to Make Yourself Available for the Master's Use

If you've been part of an evangelical church for any length of time you've probably seen it happen. The pastor brings up the subject of street witnessing, and suddenly everyone has other plans. This happens because we simply have not set aside our agendas and chosen to adopt His vision as our own. If we are not passionately sold out to God in every area opportunities will pass us by that will never come again, including many for sharing the gospel.

When you first begin to witness you may feel shy and ill-equipped. My suggestion is that you ease your way in by choosing soft targets. I will discuss the importance of choosing your targets in more details in chapter eight, sub-section two. Whatever you do—you must remain on the alert always looking for occasions to share the gospel. You may not be aware of them, but there are numerous opportunities around you every day. In addition, as you yield yourself to the Holy Spirit He will open your spiritual eyes and ears to those opportunities to share the gospel naturally and with ease, so that you soon become what I call "an opportunistic witness." The more familiar and comfortable you get with sharing the more insight you will have into the hearts of those around you, so you will be able to differentiate those who have ears to hear from those who do not—and it is those who are ready to hear I call "soft targets." That means they are open to listening to your witness. On the other hand, some are definitely not open to the gospel. Jesus explained in detail the concept of "soft targets" in **Luke 4,** when He said, "The spirit of the Lord is upon me because He has anointed me to preach the gospel to the poor, He has sent me to heal the broken hearted, to proclaim liberty to the captives and recovery of sight to the blind, to set at liberty those who are oppressed."

It is important to note that His mission was to a specific people such as the poor. Poor here does not necessarily mean financially strapped; it means poor in spirit, humble in heart. "Blessed are the poor in spirit for theirs is the kingdom of heaven." Then this passage went on to talk about the brokenhearted, those that are bruised, and those who are imprisoned. It does not mean that the gospel should not be preached to everyone; all I am saying is that in order to gain confidence, it is best to look for an opportunity to do so with someone likely to be open. Proverbs 11:30 tells us, "The fruit of righteousness is the tree of life and he that wins soul is wise." Remember, "wisdom is the principal thing." You must use the wisdom of the Holy Spirit, letting Him lead and speak through you.

6.4 Your Loudest Evangelical Voice Must Be Your Example

Witnessing is a form of leadership and the best form of leadership is always done by example. Especially in the case of family members, co-workers and close friends, they must see the witness in your life before they will listen to what you have to say, because "Actions speak louder than words." Even unbelievers and professing atheists will be watching to see if you live up to your word.

6.5 You Should Never Be Ashamed of the Gospel

Believe it or not, many people are ashamed of the gospel of Christ, although they may not readily accept that this is the case. I can recall one Sunday evening many years ago while attending a church in London, UK, the pastor decided to hold the service in front of the church building in the open air. I overheard one of the members say, "I hope my friends do not pass by and see me." I believe there are many believers like that in Christendom, but why is this so? There could be a number of reasons, but it is quite possible that such individuals may be ashamed to own Christ among their friends. The implication could also be that they did not allow their light to shine among their friends and would be made to feel awkward in such circumstances. Chances are, their friends did not know they were Christians. Then the big question is, how are we going to convince others if we have no passion for it ourselves?

6.6 Must Stay in Control and Manage Your Conversation

It is definitely not advisable to be dictatorial in your approach when witnessing; however, it is also important that you stay in control. You have to walk in authority. You have been given dominion; therefore you must stay in control.

This is not a new phenomenon; in fact, this goes to the heart of God's original intent. Let's look again at what the Bible says in **Genesis1:27–28**, "So God created man in his own image; in the image of God He created him; male and female He created them. Then God blessed them and said to them, be fruitful and multiply; fill the earth and subdue it; have dominion over the fish of the sea, over the birds of the air, and over every living thing that moves on the earth." Let me explain something here: every one of us was born to lead. Notice that in the Bible, after God said, "Let us make man in our own image and according to our likeness." His next statement was, "Let them have dominion" **(Geneses 1, v. 26).** One of the ways of reflecting God's image is by taking the lead. But let us be clear about this. The Bible did not say we are to dominate one another; it says we are to dominate over God's created order; that is over all created things. You must do whatever you can to stay in control of your conversations when witnessing.

That is, whenever you engage someone in a conversation about their salvation, make sure to keep soul-winning as your objective. In other words you will have to use wisdom, but whatever you do, do not allow your prospect to take the conversation off course. I am not suggesting that you should dictate and bully your prospect, but you must make sure the prospect remains in touch with your subject.

6.7 Be Prepared to Take It outside Your Comfort Zone

If you are going to become an expert witness for Christ, you will have to be able to speak to any and everyone from all walks of life. This notion may alarm you, but it is not as difficult as you think. Let me explain why it is necessary to be able to talk to everyone.

I have spent most of my adult life as a resident of London, United Kingdom. It is one of the most cosmopolitan cities I have ever seen. There are people from every nation, every tribe, every tongue, every religious persuasion, atheists, agnostics, etc., living in that city. It does not really matter where you live, but should you live in cities such as this, it would be of paramount importance to know how to communicate the gospel with everyone.

Living in a city such as London has provided me with the opportunity to share Christ with people from all walks of life and backgrounds. This exposure has also given me a sense of the importance of the ability to speak to people amicably, lovingly, and peaceably. Later on I will give you some practical illustrations together with some step-by-step instructions on this subject.

6.8 Must Be Determined and Persistent

As previously mentioned if you are going to become an expert in witnessing, just like anything else you will have to believe in that which you are aspiring to be, in other words, you must be driven with determination and persistence if you are going to succeed.

It is said that success is 1% inspiration and 99% perspiration. In other words, though you may be gifted and talented, you will fail if you give up or give it less than your best effort. Perhaps you've heard the old axiom that says, "The height of great men reached and kept were not attained by sudden flight, but they while their companions slept were toiling upwards through the night." You may not get there overnight, and you may not get there in the fast lane, but if you work at it, I guarantee you will become good at it. People were baffled by the ingenuity of Albert Einstein, the scientist who developed the general relativity theory, i.e., the concept of gravity and gravitational force. Some asked how he became such a genius. He said, "Because I stayed with the problem much longer."

6.9 You Will Need Spiritual Wisdom for the Task

There will be times when you will need knowledge in order to deal with some group of persons, but no need to worry—this will be a very rare circumstance. In future chapters I will share what you will need to deal with them with great knowledge. But for now, here is what the apostle has to say about the matter. "However, we speak wisdom among those who are mature, yet not the wisdom of this age, nor of the rulers of this age, who are coming to nothing. But we speak the wisdom of God in a mystery, the hidden *wisdom* which God ordained before the ages for our glory, which none of the rulers of this age knew; for had they known, they would not have crucified the Lord of glory" **(1 Corinthians 2:8).**

Here is what **Proverbs 2**, has to say about it.

> "My son, if you receive my words and treasure my commandments within you, so that you incline your ears to wisdom and apply your heart to understanding. Yes, if you cry out for discernment and lift up your voice for understanding. If you seek her as silver and search for her as for hidden treasure, then you will understand the fear of the Lord. And find the knowledge of God. For the Lord gives wisdom; from His mouth comes knowledge and understanding. He stores up sound wisdom for the uprightly; He is a shield to those who walk uprightly; He guards the path of justice, and preserves the way of His saints. Then you will understand righteousness and justice, equity and every good path. When wisdom enters your heart, and knowledge is pleasant to your soul,"
>
> and note this,
>
> "Discretion will preserve you; and understanding will keep you," and it went on to say that "To deliver you from the way of evil, from the man who speaks perverse things."

Having wisdom will assist you in dealing with the different people and situations you will encounter. Remember, "Wisdom is the principal thing."

Chapter Checklist

In review:

- To become a master of personal evangelism, you will need a desire to want to do it.
- You have to be pregnant with a burden for souls.
- If you don't already possess this burden you can begin to pray it in.
- You must be someone who has an aptitude for the study of God's word.
- Must walk worthy of Christ.
- Must be available for the Master's use.
- Must set a good example.
- Should never be ashamed of the gospel of Christ.
- Have to learn how to stay in control of your conversations. This means you should not allow your prospect to get off topic.
- Should aim to take the gospel beyond your local surroundings.
- You must be determined and persistent not allowing any negative experiences to prevent you from doing God's business.
- You will need spiritual wisdom.

------------------------------- Questions ---------------------------------

1. Name five of the nine ways given in this chapter to prepare you to witness.

2. What kind of debates you should avoid at all cost?

3. Why are we called to walk worthy of Christ?

4. What is the most common reaction from believers about witnessing?

5. What is the best approach to take when starting out as a witness?

6. What is described as your loudest evangelical voice?

7. What percentage of inspiration and perspiration are required for success?

---

8. Complete this sentence: Commitment will allow the Holy Spirit to lead you to...

---

9. What kind of wisdom will you need if you are going to master personal evangelism?

Personal Notes

SECTION 3

Practical Steps to Overcome and Master the Challenges of Personal Evangelism

Chapters 7 - 12

= CHAPTER SEVEN =

Dealing with the Fear Factor

On one of my missionary journeys to the United States, I was asked by a bishop to take his church for an evening of evangelism. Prompted by the spirit, I decided to have a group discussion instead of a preaching session. I wanted to interact with the people to get an understanding of their perspectives on the subject.

Prior to the meeting, I decided to make a random list of what I believed to be the main problems. After organizing the group and introducing the subject, I began by asking the congregants to tell me what they thought were the main factors preventing people from actively engaging in personal evangelism. The answers they gave were astounding, strikingly similar to the list I had made earlier.

The first answer I received was fear. This also happens to be at the top of my list. The person answering went on to say that the fear of rejection was her biggest hindrance.

Another attendee asked about how to initiate contact. For example, if you were taking a stroll in the park one day and saw a person or group of people, how would you approach them and bring up the subject of their eternity?

How to answer difficult questions—another important point raised at the meeting...

What do you do when someone with whom you are sharing the gospel asks you questions for which you do not have the answers?

If you are someone who has problems when it comes to personal evangelism, I am sure that your reason falls into the category above. In which case, I would like to show you how simple it is to approach someone without fear and how to answer difficult questions with ease.

7.1 Fear – Your Biggest Enemy

I am sure that you have found yourself in a situation where you would like to witness to someone about Christ but found that you are consumed with fear.

Perhaps you're fearful of where and how to begin and your mind races as you wonder what they will think and whether they will reject you. If you have ever found yourself in that situation, do not despair—we have all been there. In fact, human beings are afraid of many things. For example, some fear heights, some fear the dark, and it is said that some even fear success—but one of mankind's greatest fears is the fear of rejection.

In this section I will show you how to witness with confidence, but I must warn you that, like any other skill, conquering fear is a process and will not necessarily happen overnight.

So what is fear?

Recently I heard what is to me, one of the best definitions of fear I've ever heard, an acronym:

False

Evidence

Appearing

Real

Fear is a powerful thing—a tool the enemy uses, that can actually capture the mind and cause false reality to appear real. For example, while I was attending work experience in fulfillment of my school finals in Montego Bay, Jamaica, we needed to get from Catherine Hall to the downtown area of Montego Bay during our lunch hour. Barnet Street was the long way around, so we took a shortcut across a train bridge that took only a few minutes. It was not paved, and was covered by planks of wood with huge gaps between the planks. My friends would simply run across the bridge, but I was terrified, totally gripped with fear, even when my cousin allowed me to hold onto him. To me it seemed the gaps between the planks were gigantic and I could slip through into the river, though the reality was quite different. Unfortunately, because of my fears I usually ended up taking the long way up Barnet Street.

If the truth were to be known, most of us have our own share of fears, especially where witnessing is concerned. The only difference is that over time and with encouragement some of us have overcome it.

7.2 Fear of Rejection

The fear of rejection is the greatest hindrance of all when it comes to sharing our faith.

When we speak of fear of rejection, we are speaking of the "irrational fear that others will not accept us for who we are, what we believe and how we behave." This kind of irrational fear will definitely cause us to be cautious in our behavior and interaction with others, and it can be paralyzing in nature. It is usually birthed out of a lack of confidence and often happens to those who are overly dependent on the approval, recognition, and affirmation of others in order to feel good about themselves. This is usually what keeps us from being ourselves. These people are so driven by the need for acceptance that they often lose their identity in the process. They are usually followers and do not make good leaders or good witnesses. If you want to become an effective witness you must learn to set your fear aside and become a leader.

In order to keep from falling into this kind of trap I constantly remind myself that nobody's opinion of me is my reality—that God's opinion is the only one that counts. For those of you who struggle with fear of rejection, this is a good mindset to adopt. Whenever you are confronted with fear of rejection, you should repeat this phrase, "Nobody's opinion of me is my reality." In other words, you do not have to agree with anyone else's opinion of you.

Suppose I were to tell you that if you are always concerned about people's opinions, you will never be able to live a successful spiritual life. Here is what the Bible says: "For do I now persuade men, or God? Or do I seek to please men? For if I still pleased men, I would not be a bondservant of Christ" **(Galatians 1, v. 10)**. **1 Thessalonians 2:4** says, "But as we have been approved by God to be entrusted with the gospel, even so we speak, not as pleasing men, but God who tests our hearts."

But as we have been approved by God to be entrusted with the gospel, even so we speak, not as pleasing men, but God who tests our hearts.

We cannot seek the approval of men above the approval of God and please Him. In fact, Scripture actually calls such a man double-minded in all his ways. As human beings, we are naturally drawn to the praise of others. We love being complimented and honored. And there's nothing intrinsically wrong with that. At least not until it becomes so important that it takes precedence over everything else. Jesus addressed this issue in Matthew 6:1: "Take heed that you do not do your charitable deeds before men, to be seen by them. Otherwise you have no reward from your father in heaven." It's clear that our first priority should be the approval of God rather than the approval of men.

7.2.2 Peer Pressure

Fear of rejection is also a result of peer pressure.

Peer pressure is influence exerted on us by a person or group of persons in order to get us to do something we would not otherwise do. When we suffer from the fear of rejection, it can cause us to act out of character. It can cause us to crave recognition from the peer group with which we want to be identified, and prevent us from taking the initiative to do anything outside that world. It could also prevent us from taking the initiative to do things for ourselves or for the kingdom of God.

7.3 How Does Fear Affect Us?

Anywhere there is fear, you will also find doubt. So the question is: How can you be convincing when you doubt it yourselves? Fear will change our behavior as well as the behavior of others toward us, which will inadvertently prevent us from being effective.

7.4 Fear Affects Behavior

Usually, people who act out of the fear of rejection display little or no assertiveness. For example, they will not speak up and let others know how they feel about issues, especially if they are of a different opinion.

They do not naturally operate out of confidence. They are unable to encourage themselves, let alone anyone else. They lack the capacity to function independently, and often resort to passive and occasionally aggressive behavior and do not tend to communicate openly. They have a tendency to disguise their true feelings. They will always be in tune with what is in and out of fashion and will make every effort to emulate that in their lives. In private, they will frequently express anger over their current situation. Any effort to assist or encourage them will be met by confrontation, because they are confused by their lack of identity and wear masks to please others. They are usually rigid and inflexible.

It's not hard to see how counterproductive such behavior is. As a consequence Christians cannot afford to operate out of the fear of rejection. When you walk into a room, you should immediately feel that you are comfortable in your own skin and able to handle any situation. At the same time it's important to fend off any sense of pride. Confidence does not mean you should be overbearing or pushy. After all, you are a servant of God, which requires that the higher you rise, the more subservient you become.

Did you know that when you act out of fear, the very thing you fear is likely to happen to you? **Job 3:25:** "For the thing I greatly feared has come upon me, and what I dreaded has happened to me." That is why it is said that "the only thing to fear is fear itself." You will likely encounter two types of reactions when acting out of fear: those who love and care for you and those who are eager to exploit you.

7.4.1 Those That Care for You

Those who care about you are likely to encourage you to be more positive and assertive. They may even ask you to make some changes to your approach and to be as real as possible. If you are not assertive, you will come across as hypocritical and insincere. If your demeanor implies insincerity, even those who love you will find it hard to trust your integrity and honesty. They may become turned off by your behavior, which they know to be unreal.

Those who love and want to help you will eventually become frustrated if you ignore or reject their offers for help. They may even become anxious around you, because they can't read your hidden emotions. At some point they may give up on you, because they see that you have chosen to remain stuck in a self-defeating cycle. In the end they may even avoid you because it's easier than dealing with your issues.

Those who operate out of fear of rejection can end up pushing away the very ones who love and wish to help. When these people pull away it can feel like rejection and can even aggravate an already bad situation.

7.4.2 Some Will Take Advantage of You

Can you imagine trying to share the gospel with someone who wants to exploit you? This is what this second group of persons will do to you if you operate out of the fear of rejection. They begin by taking you for granted, because you fail to stand up for yourself. They will soon realize that you are making great sacrifices to gain their acceptance, and take great joy in ignoring you and even making your life miserable. Ultimately there is a great likelihood that they will apply pressure on you to conform to their way of life. And if you're anxious to conform they will not be open to your proposals regarding the gospel, because they will see you as insincere and unstable. The bottom line is, the moment they become aware that you are motivated by the fear of rejection they will never take you seriously. Over time they will begin to reject you entirely. Can you see why it is a virtual impossibility to operate out of fear of rejection and communicate the gospel convincingly? This is a classical example, as Job said, of having the very thing you fear happening to you. This can sometimes lead to manipulation— meaning they may openly reject you once they have used you and feel they no longer need you.

It means then, that if you operate out of fear of rejection you could end up being rejected by the very people from whom you fear rejection.

7.5 Why Do People Operate Out of Fear of Rejection?

People act out of the fear of rejection because:

- They lack healthy self-esteem. This is usually because they were never fully affirmed in their family of origin.
- They may have had a traumatic experience of rejection in the past that deeply scarred them.
- They may be bound up in traditional thinking and have come to realize that, that kind of behavior is neither rational nor necessary.

- It could be that they also lacked appropriate role models who accepted them for who they really were, resulting in an ongoing lack of confidence in their own abilities.
- They may be insecure in their personal identity, resulting in a serious lack of self-confidence within interpersonal relationships.
- They might never have been exposed to healthy ways of dealing with conflicts or disagreements.
- They may have lacked the social skills to adapt to a reference group.
- They may have suffered from social isolation in their early lives.
- They may have failed at personal accomplishments, which make them feel inadequate.
- They operate out of fear of rejection but may even deny it if it is pointed out to them.
- They may have a physical condition that they feel makes them unattractive to others
- They may have been told all their lives that they were not good enough or were different.

7.6 Steps to Overcoming the Fear of Rejection

If you are someone who has suffered from fear of rejection, fear must be conquered in order to master the art of personal evangelism. That is the bad news; the good news is that with a little help and some basic guidelines, you can do it. You have to conquer fear because on the one hand, fear is not of God. See **2 Timothy 1:7**. "For God has not given us a spirit of fear, but of power and of love and of a sound mind." The term "sound mind" denotes good judgment, a disciplined thought pattern, and the ability to understand and make wise decisions using self-control and self-discipline. It means that if you are going to share the gospel, you must be disciplined and self-controlled. The Bible says the letter kills, so it's wise to remember that you don't just share the gospel with what you say, but by the genuine sincerity of your words. In other words, people have to feel what you say.

Here are some steps to take to overcome the fear of rejection:

1. Under no circumstances should you ever take things personally. If you tend to take things personally and are easily offended by what people say, you are going to have difficulty. If you name the name of Christ, you will be made to feel offended at times, but keep in mind that it is not you the devil is mad with—it's the Christ that is in you.

2. Try to define yourself independently of other people's opinions. For example, if you are someone who likes to help, avoid thinking about other people's reactions. When you care too much about what other people think, you will be open to manipulation. When you don't care about what other people think, you are more likely to be honest because you do not have to pretend so much.

3. Try to become comfortable being uncomfortable. If you are rejected, take it as a challenge and learn to accept the situation. "Rejection is a word, the fear of rejection is a feeling, overcoming fear of rejection is an action, and action speaks louder than words."

The first step to conquering fear of witnessing is to speak out. **2 Timothy 1:8** says, "Be not thou therefore ashamed of the testimony of our Lord." Sometimes we need to kill the demon called fear by simply doing the thing we fear most, in this case, by speaking out. Believe me, when I say that people may not be as difficult to talk to as first perceived. I mean it. I challenge you to take the initiative and watch the outcome.

7.7 You Must be Sold on Your Mission

If you are going to conquer fear you will have to be sold on your mission, in other words you have to have total confidence in what you are offering. As mentioned earlier, to become successful at selling anything you must believe in what you are selling. That is not necessarily the same as being sold out to your religion. And also as I have said on occasion, some people are totally sold out to a religious belief but not sold out the same way about their faith in Jesus. You can easily measure this by their conversation. They will speak much about what their religion teaches rather than pointing souls to the cross. Don't waste your time by making this mistake. Even Jesus did not conform to the religious order of His day. If you are totally sold out for Christ, it will not be difficult to impart what you have to offer to the lost and dying.

7.8 You Must Believe in Yourself

In addition to believing in your mission, you must also believe in yourself. Now don't get me wrong. Under no circumstances should you rely on your own strength or your own ability. Once again, "Wisdom is the principal thing; in all thy getting get understanding." Scripture also says we are not to lean on our own understanding. To believe in yourself is to believe in the One who is your source. Remember, you can do all things through Christ who strengthens you.

The starting point has to be that you are totally committed to following Jesus. Notice I did not say that you have to be perfect, but you do have to be committed. Once you are fully committed, you will soon discover the Lord has not given you a spirit of fear but of power and of a sound mind. This does not mean that you will not feel fearful or intimidated at times, but you will always find the courage to triumph and to accomplish whatever you have set out to achieve.

7.9 A Practical Way to Deal with Fear

To help you deal with your fear let me share an example from my own experience. As previously mentioned it helps me to deal with fear when I think of myself as an opportunistic witness. It's a great place to start and works every time. I begin by looking for people with whom I can share Christ. These are people who may need help and support and, as such, will be more receptive to the gospel. And while it may be your ultimate aim to win the world for Christ, why not start with those who will listen to what you say? The truth is that not everyone is ready or open to the gospel, but it is far easier if you find someone with whom you can at least open a dialogue. Once again, please do not get me wrong. Everyone you meet provides an opportunity for ministry; however, you must be aware that not all will be receptive. Not only that, but, time and place may be of some relevance as well, simply put, make sure the time and place is convenient. The big question then is, how will you know who will be receptive and who will not? We will discuss these things in the next chapter.

Chapter Checklist

In Review

In this chapter we have discussed the necessary steps to take to master the art of personal evangelism.

- The first thing you have to do is conquer fear.
- You must be confident about your mission.
- The only thing to fear is fear itself.
- Fear is nothing more than false evidence that appears real.
- The main thing people fear is rejection.
- Fear will affect your behavior.
- In order to deal with fear of rejection you must:
    - Never take offense personally.
    - Try to define yourself independently and never allow anybody's opinion of you to become your reality.
    - Try to be comfortable being uncomfortable.
    - You must learn to speak out.
- Learn to believe in yourself without relying on your own strength or ability.

--------------------------------- Questions ---------------------------------

1. What is the main reason why most people do not witness?

2. Name two types of fear that prevent people from witnessing.

3. Explain the acronym—F.E.A.R.

4. What motto might help you combat fear?

5. Name at least three ways that fear is likely to affect you.

6. What two types of reactions are you likely to encounter if you act out of fear of rejection?

7. According to **2 Timothy 1:7**, what kind of spirit has God not given us?

___

8. Name 3 steps to overcoming the fear of rejection.

___

Personal Notes

= CHAPTER EIGHT =

How to Initiate Contact

You may have been walking in the park one day and had the urge to share the gospel but had no idea how to go about it. If so, you are not alone. As I mentioned earlier there are many who have never won a single soul to Christ, because they simply do not feel comfortable taking that first step.

So how do you approach someone with the gospel? Herein lies one of the greatest hurdles you must cross, if you are going to master the art of personal evangelism. In my opinion, this may be one of the most important chapters in the book. I say that because if you can master the art of initiating contact, you will have inadvertently conquered fear as well.

Here are some simple basic rules that will help you put that fear to rest.

8.1 Rule Number 1 - Change Your Language

Let's begin at home or closer to home and then move further afield. In order to initiate a conversation with people you are already familiar with, you must change the way you talk. Upon becoming a Christian, your conversation must be different.

In Ephesians 2 the apostle Paul reminds us that we once "walked according to the course of this world, according to the prince of the power of the air, the spirit who now works in the sons of disobedience; among whom also we all once conducted ourselves in the lusts of our flesh, fulfilling the desires of the flesh and the mind, and were by nature children of wrath, even as the others."

Notice that one of the things Paul addressed was the way we used to speak. Before becoming Christians, we had our conversation "in the lust of the flesh fulfilling the desires of the flesh and of the mind." But now that we have believed in the Lord Jesus Christ, we are to be followers of Him. That means we must walk and talk like Jesus, even using what we might call a heavenly language.

Simply put, now that we are Christians, we no longer use profanity, slang and questionable clichés. Here Paul is saying we should change the way we speak. I could even take it a little further than this. For example, instead of just saying thank you, how about saying, "God bless you." I know you may be thinking, "So what is wrong with saying, "thank you"? Of course, nothing is wrong with saying thank you, but if you say "God bless you," you are sending a message to that person that you believe and trust in God. Let's try another one: suppose a friend says, "My manager is really pressuring me, and I'm finding it difficult to cope." How about offering your support by saying something like, "I will remember you in my prayers." And perhaps they would permit you to pray out loud right then. Or, if someone is ill you could say, "May I pray for you?"

Notice that by doing these things you are not Bible-bashing anyone or having to disrupt anyone's activities. By simply changing the way you speak, you can get their attention. Don't be too worried about the result or the response. It may be years later that someone will be in trouble and in need of help and somebody will say, "So and so is a Christian, and you can ask her to pray for you." Using that kind of spiritual language will go a long way toward making and establishing contacts in the course of your daily routine.

8.2 Rule Number 2 - Choose Your Targets

> It is important that you choose your targets with wisdom

As you move out to talk to perfect strangers, the first thing I want you to understand is that until you have become more proficient in sharing the gospel, and especially for those with very little experience, it is important that you realize that not everyone will receive the gospel. That's why we discussed in chapter six sub-section three that it's important to choose your targets. In this section we will discuss the importance of choosing your targets carefully. Simply put, don't go trying to talk to everybody you meet about Christ until you are able to do so expertly; choose your targets with wisdom. Here's why I say this: Can you imagine, approaching and trying to discuss the general relativity theory or the big-bang concept with an atheist science nerd? To make matters worse, assume that these are subjects with which you have no prior knowledge and these are people who are well-educated in those areas. If you fail to choose your targets wisely your efforts may be a dismal failure making you hesitant to ever try to witness again.

As you begin sharing the gospel, whatever you do, do not take on more than you can handle. It is strongly advisable to wait until you have some experience under your belt as to how to talk to them. We will discuss this in more detail in the next chapter, but for now don't allow your zeal and enthusiasm to get the better of you; you must start small and stay in control.

8.3 Rule Number 3 -Find a Need and Fill It

In my opinion, one of the most effective ways of witnessing to anyone—whether close to home or a perfect stranger is to simply find a need and meet it. If you look around you will find needs everywhere. Believe it or not, most people you meet on a daily basis could use your support in some way. You do not even need to go out of your way if you do not want to. Remember, from a kingdom perspective, every great person in the kingdom possesses the heart and spirit of a servant. I know that for some of you, this may be contrary to what you already believe. You may have always associated greatness to those with special gifts, such as those with the gift of the gab, the educated, and the wealthy, but that is not according to Scripture.

Hear me on this—this is no new phenomenon. Jesus said, "He that will be great in the kingdom let him be your servant." In other words, he is willing to serve. And though you should pay special attention to the development of all aspects of your life, once again, you do not need eloquence of speech nor any such thing to be of service to God. All you have to do is see someone in need and lend a helping hand. Filling a need is one of the easiest and best ways to get someone's attention. This will almost always present the opportunity for sharing the gospel. (See illustration of the Good Samaritan below). On this point alone I guarantee you will return in a week recounting how many people with whom you have comfortably and joyfully shared the gospel.

> And though you should pay special attention to the development of all aspects of your life, you do not need eloquence of speech to be of service to God.

As we have already established, it is best to get your practice with those at home first before you take your message abroad. Therefore, start with your family, your friends, and your neighbors. All you have to do is look for that senior citizen or that pregnant woman who needs help. This is not some complicated theological or philosophical concept; it is something everyone can and should do.

Remember that your salvation is not just fire insurance for you as you're waiting to go to heaven; rather we are told to "occupy until He comes." The Bible has placed a very strong emphasis on loving God and our neighbor as ourselves. Why then should you not want your neighbor to come into the same knowledge of God that you have?

The question here then is, how do you go about doing this? Let me ask you this: Do you know how powerful a pleasant word and a smile can be to most people you meet on a daily basis? Under no circumstance should a Christian walk around looking depressed or sad. I am not oblivious to the fact that we do go through difficulties from time to time; however, we should still have joy. **Galatians 5:22-23** says, "But the fruit of the Spirit is love, joy, peace, longsuffering, kindness, goodness, faithfulness, gentleness, self-control. Against such there is no law." Because the joy of the Lord is our strength we, more than anyone else, should have peace that the world can't give.

A pleasant personality together with a passionate love for God and for your neighbor should prepare you to initiate a contact, but first answer this question:

8.4 Who is your Neighbor?

Many people consider their neighbors to be only those who live next door or those in their neighborhoods. But Scripture does not agree. Luke 10 provides a perfect illustration as to who your neighbor really is. Verse 25 says, "And behold a certain lawyer stood up and tested Him." Listen to me—if they tested Jesus, we too will be tested. The lawyer tested him saying, "Teacher, what shall I do to inherit eternal life?" Jesus said to him, "What is written in the Law? What is your reading of it?" So he answered and said, "You shall love the Lord your God with all your heart, with all your soul, with all your strength and with all your mind, and your neighbor as yourself." If you love God you will make yourself available to help anyone who needs it wherever you meet them. And He (Jesus) said to Him, "You have answered rightly; do this and you will live." But the man, who wanted to justify himself, asked, "And who is my neighbor?'"

It was here that Jesus responded by telling the story of the Good Samaritan. "Then Jesus answered and said; A certain man went down from Jerusalem to Jericho and fell among thieves who stripped him of his clothing, wounded him and departed leaving him half dead. Now by chance a certain priest came down that road. And when he saw him he passed by on the other side." Notice that the first person who passed by was the priest (the bishop of the church) but he showed absolutely no compassion on the man; in fact, he passed by on the other side of the street. "Likewise, a Levite"—now this is the assistant pastor—"when he arrived at the place, came and looked, and passed by on the other side." Notice that the Levite actually came and looked at the man, but the Bible said he also went on his way. Wasn't that a great opportunity for ministry? I believe it was, however, both the priest and the Levite ignored the opportunity. "But a certain Samaritan, as he journeyed came where he was. And when he saw him, he had compassion, so he went to him and bandaged his wounds, pouring in oil and wine; and he set him on his own animal, brought him to an inn, and took care of him. On the next day when he departed, he took out two denarii (coins), gave them to the inn keeper, and said to him, take care of him and whatever more you spend, when I come again, I will repay you." Jesus then said to the lawyer, "So which of these three do you think was neighbor to him that fell among thieves? And he said, he who showed mercy on him. Then Jesus said to him, go and do likewise." We also should go and do as the Good Samaritan did.

How do you suppose the injured man would've reacted had he once again met the Samaritan? I believe he would've felt deep gratitude toward him, don't you? Now let's imagine the Samaritan was a worshiper of God. Do you think he would be afraid to invite the man to his place of worship? I don't think so—and the man? I believe he would, no doubt, have eagerly accepted the invitation, and perhaps come to salvation in Christ. Do you see what a good deed can do? Well, is there any reason why you shouldn't go and do likewise? I don't think so.

Let me emphasize once again that when witnessing you should not be too concerned about the outcome. Remember, "Paul planted, Apollos watered but God gave the increase."

But let us not be too quick to move on from here. It is imperative for you to appreciate the real reason why this story came about. I believe that **Luke 10** is one of the most significant evangelistic passages in the Bible. In fact, it all started in Chapter 9 when Jesus called his twelve disciples together and gave them power and authority over demons, and to cure diseases. He sent them to preach the kingdom of God and to heal the sick. "And He said to them, "Take nothing for your journey, neither staffs nor bag nor bread nor money; and do not have two tunics apiece. Whatever house you enter, stay there, and from there depart. And whosoever will not receive you, when you go out of that city shake off the very dust from your feet as a testimony against them.'" Please note that when sharing the gospel you will not always be well-received. As Jesus said of His disciples, so it will be for you too—some will put you out of their houses, out of their cities and even out of their churches. But here I must emphasize that whether they accept you or not you are to be "steadfast, immovable, always abounding in the works of the Lord." Notice what Jesus did in Luke, Chapter 9. He sent His disciples out two by two for some on-the-job training. Especially when you are just starting out, it may be helpful to go out in the company of others. Perhaps go with those who are more experienced and comfortable in their role as a witness. Maybe this is something we can learn from the Jehovah's Witnesses; they go out in pairs, a senior person with a trainee.

And while prior preparation is a good and necessary thing, such on-the-job-training can make up for any deficits in your education. That is what is meant by the phrase, "thrown into the deep end." Notice that the first thing He did was to motivate them by calling them together for a time of impartation. He gave them power and authority. He then gave them specific direction. It is of vital importance that you follow the pattern God laid down for ministry.

8.5 Rule Number 4 - Establish the Basis for the Conversation

When you go out to witness, if possible, be the first to speak. This will let you set the tone and determine the direction of the conversation. No matter how it may first appear people are nearly always willing to talk if someone will take the initiative and be sincere, pleasant and kind. Once again, be careful not to go overboard, because you will come across as insincere.

It's also important to give people the impression that you are interested in them personally and that they are not merely a "religious project." Just as the Good Samaritan did, we must meet the basic physical needs of the person in order to open the door to their hearts.

If you live in large cities such as London, New York, or Tokyo, you will find that it is not always easy for people to appreciate even a friendly gesture from others, because everyone seems to be a suspect. Despite this, however, if you make some effort, you will find that most will respond to a kind word or a kind gesture. For example, I find that if I walk into a room or even on the street and say something like, "How are you today?" I will almost always get a positive response, even in big cities.

As it was in the story of the "Good Samaritan" it is best to start with those who have obvious needs. Say, for example, that you are at a bus stop and you observe a lady with a pram trying to board the bus. Ask, "May I assist you?" It would be a rare thing for her to say no. Or perhaps you run across someone with an unusual feature that most people would stare at or turn away from. You could ask how they are and show compassion. I guarantee that most would be happy to connect with you if you show genuine compassion. In fact, such situations are regular occurrences in my life.

For example, one morning as I was at the train station on my way to work in London UK, I observed a relatively young-looking lady who appeared to have some form of disability perhaps from a misfortune in her early life. From her countenance it was clear that she was very unhappy, but, during that rare rush hour connection, I smiled at her and said, "How are you today?" She did not respond too kindly at that moment, but when we met at the train the next day she apologized, saying she had had a really bad day and did not immediately realize I was just trying to be kind to her. That right there presented a powerful ministry opportunity.

Again, one day I was in a large store in the United States when I observed an older Jewish lady walking with some difficulty. I asked, "How are you today?" and as she explained about her aches and pains, I asked, "May I pray for you?" She responded in stunned disbelief. "Will you really pray for me?" I responded, "Right here and now." Right there in an open public place, I laid my hand on her and prayed in the name of JESUS.

Another time I went to the hospital in London, UK, where an Asian man lay in bed, next to the person I had gone to visit. I did not investigate, but he appeared to be of Indian or Pakistani origin, in which case he was probably Muslim, Hindu, or Sikh. That did not matter to me, and upon ending my prayers for the other man I went to him and asked, "Sir, would you like me to pray for you?" He was dying of cancer, and of course he was delighted. I prayed in the name of Jesus, the only name by which men shall be saved.

This point could not be better illustrated than it is in John 4, where Jesus ministered to the woman at the well. Notice that this woman had a need. She was obviously a "snubbed gender within a despised race." The women of her town probably did not keep company with her because she had a reputation, and hence she was alone at the well. Other Jews would not even speak to her because of her race. But notice that Jesus spoke to her because He was different. We as Christians must be different from everybody else. Jesus spoke first; He did not isolate himself even from those others saw as unworthy.

> Therefore, when the Lord knew that the Pharisees had heard that Jesus made and baptized more disciples than John (although Jesus himself did not baptize, but His disciples) He left Judea and departed again to Galilee. But He needed to go through Samaria. So He came to a city of Samaria which is called Sychar, near the plot of ground that Jacob gave to his son Joseph. Now Jacob's well was there. Jesus therefore being wearied from His journey, sat thus by the well, it was about the sixth hour. A woman

> of Samaria came to draw water, Jesus said to her, "Give me a drink." **John 4:1-7**

It is my considered opinion that if you take the initiative to speak first, it will give you the psychological advantage to decide what line of conversation to pursue. If you have ever been approached by someone trying to start a conversation you know that it's hard to turn the tide to witness. So be sure to take the initiative so you can stay in control.

8.4 Rule Number 5 - Establish a Common Ground

Having taken the initiative to speak first, the next thing you must do is to establish a common ground. The importance of establishing a common ground cannot be overstated, because your conversation must be relevant to the situation of the moment. Notice that in His chat with the woman at the well, Jesus connected with her over a similar interest—water. Jesus asked her to give Him a drink.

> For His disciple had gone away into the city to buy food. Then the woman said to Him, "How is it that you being a Jew, ask a drink from me being a Samaritan woman? For the Jews have no dealings with the Samaritans. Jesus said to her, "If you know the gift of God, and who it is who says to you, give Me a drink, you would have asked him and He would have given you living water." The woman said to Him, "Sir, you have nothing to draw with, and the well is deep. Where then do you get the living water? Are you greater than our father Jacob, who gave us the well, and drank from it himself, as well as his sons and his livestock?" Jesus answered and said to her, "Whosoever drinks of this water will thirst again, but whosoever drinks of the water I shall give him will never thirst.

> But the water that I shall give him, will become in him a fountain of water springing up into everlasting life." The woman said to him; "Sir, give me this living water, that I may not thirst, nor come here to draw." **John 4:8-15**

Notice how Jesus established that common ground. He could have said something like, "I am Jesus the Christ, and I can give you living water so you will never thirst again." Maybe that is what most of us would have done—instantly displaying our credentials. I am pastor so-and-so or evangelist so-and-so, in an effort to create an impression. But Jesus did not do that. He simply aroused interest by discussing something of interest to her. The woman of Samaria responded, "How is it that you being a Jew ask a drink of me, a Samaritan woman? For Jews have no dealings with Samaritans."

After you have established a common ground, it is important that you listen and understand what they are telling you and use that as a basis for what you want to communicate to them. In other words, trade punches on their territory, not on yours. I know that you may not readily appreciate this, so let me tell you what I mean and then share a couple of my own examples.

What I mean is this: In order for you to engage someone in an effective conversation, you must first get their attention. Otherwise it will be impossible to get your message across. What am I saying? I'm saying that the best way to do this is to get them talking. People like to hear their own voices most of all, while listening is an art; it shows intelligence and concern. There is an old proverb that says, "A fool is known by his much speaking." In other words, you can only reveal the lack of knowledge when you open your mouth. **Proverbs 12:23** also said, "A prudent man conceals knowledge, but the heart of fools proclaim foolishness." Chapter 23:9 says: "Do not speak in the hearing of a fool, for he will despise the wisdom of your words."

Remember, once you have established a common ground, you must be as pleasant as possible and allow the other person to speak. Never lose sight of the fact that you are an ambassador for Christ, and you should never misrepresent the kingdom.

8.5 Rule Number 6 - Must Arouse Interest

If someone tries to engage you in a conversation in which you have absolutely no interest, how would you react? If you are of a bold personality, you might tell them to get lost. On the other hand, if you are someone who is careful of other people's feelings, you may prefer to stay and listen responding with the occasional, "Yeah, right." "Okay," etc. But even if you are of a compassionate nature, your body language may still paint a picture that says, "Can't you see that I am not interested?"

Well, this is the kind of reaction you are likely to get if you attempt to share the gospel with someone who is not interested. And, if that is the case you must find a way to arouse their interest—in order to establish that common ground. Remember that the outcome is not your concern. Your responsibility is to share and let God bring the increase. Do not, for one moment, be tempted to force your opinion on the other person, because even God allows men to have their own free will.

This is the mistake they made in the churches of twenty to thirty years ago. We were bombarded with fire and brimstone messages that frightened us into becoming Christians. Inasmuch as that may have its place, what this failed to do, was to teach us how to develop a hunger and a love for God. As a result, as soon as the fear factor wore off many left the church. In essence, fear, in and of itself, is not a strong enough motivator to produce passion. The point I am making is that if you are consumed with a passion and love for God, it will inevitably provide you with authentic and unmistakable platforms that will arouse the interest of others. Trust me—even the most hardened heathen will be able to grasp your passion for God. Your lifestyle will speak volumes so they sense that you have something that is missing from their lives.

Once again, St. John 4 provides a classic example of how Jesus aroused the interest of the Samaritan woman. Notice what Jesus did. He literally made the woman at the well feel that something was missing. He did this by making her thirsty for something more than water. The question to ask then is: how can you get someone to come to the point of wanting what you have to offer? The answer is, you have to be consumed with the inner consciousness that it is a must-have. Here is what I mean: If you are not totally committed to your faith and your walk with God, how then are you going to convince someone they must have what you've got—that is, if you do not appear to be driven with your own passion for it?

This was what Jesus did. He led her down a path that opened the flood gate of her need for that which He was offering. "Jesus answered and said to her, 'Whoever drinks of this water will thirst again, but whoever drinks of the water that I shall give him will never thirst. But the water that I shall give him will become in him a fountain of water springing up into everlasting life.' The woman said to Him, 'Sir, give me this water, that I may not thirst, nor come here to draw.'" All Jesus did was engage her in a casual conversation about a drink of water. You do not have to be too deep or too steeped in Hebrew and Greek to convince someone of the need for salvation.

Chapter Checklist

To review: The rules for initiating contact include:

- Changing the way you speak by simply using terms such as, "God bless you," "I will pray for you," etc.
- Adopting an attitude of helping especially for those in particular need.
- Taking the initiative to be the first to speak so that you can set the tone of the conversation.
- The importance of establishing a common, ground, i.e. making your conversations relevant to the person, situation and circumstances.
- The need to arouse interest, citing the well-known story of Jesus and the "woman at the well."

-------------------------------- Questions ---------------------------------

1. Name three basic rules for how to initiate contacts.

2. What famous Bible story was used to illustrate the question regarding who is our neighbor?

3. When Jesus asked the lawyer who of the three persons was neighbor to the man who fell among thieves, what was the lawyer's answer?

4. In your own words describe the lesson you can learn from the lawyer's reply.

5. What was Jesus' instruction to the lawyer?

6. What did Jesus send His disciples to do in Luke Chapter 9?

7. What 2 important things did Jesus give to the disciples?

---

8. When sharing the gospel, you will be well-received by everyone. True/False

---

9. When sharing the gospel, you should show people you are only interested in the spiritual. True/False

---

10. Name two things you need to show when initiating contact.

---

11. What familiar interest did Jesus use when establishing a common ground with the woman at the well?

---

12. How did He do this?

Personal Notes

= CHAPTER NINE =

How to Deal with Difficult Questions

The chances are that at some time nearly everyone has talked with someone with a serious appetite for philosophy. The word "philosophy" actually means a love for knowledge. People with that bent tend to want to impress others at every opportunity. Their views are often twisted, especially in regard to religion. This is true even among Christians. An excellent illustration can be found in Colossians Chapter three, where Paul wrote concerning false teaching that was creeping into the church. They had started to teach Greek philosophy and Jewish legalism, which were in essence undermining the authenticity of Christ and threatening to bring confusion and false teaching into the church. This occurred because of the Greeks' love for knowledge and hence, resulted in a distorted view of what a Christian should be. These kinds of people tend to want to prove themselves by posing difficult questions.

As an amateur witness you've probably wondered how to handle such difficult questions. Perhaps the thought makes you feel anxious. If so, let me reassure you that there is no need to be afraid. In the next few paragraphs I will show you how to deal with any tough questions you are likely to encounter.

But first, let me remind you that you have nothing to prove when witnessing, because as I have said to you on occasion in this book, it's not about you or even about man's wisdom. The wisdom that you require to carry out the task comes from God. Remember that in Luke 9 Jesus told His disciples not to take anything with them, why?—because the Holy Spirit would give them the exact words to say, when they needed it. The Holy Spirit is the supreme and unseen witness; you are only a vessel through which He pours His anointing. That however, does not mean you should not seek to know your subject. Let me remind you once again that **2 Timothy 2:15** says, "Study to show yourself approved unto God, a workman who needs not to be ashamed, rightly dividing the word of truth." We must remember that the Bible is the inspired Word of God, and being well-versed equips us with confidence as the Holy Spirit anoints us to witness. It is His written instruction to mankind, and provides an answer for every important question in life. It explains the way of salvation as well as providing instructions for how to live. Therefore, every Christian witness ought to be a student of the Word. That is what Paul admonished Timothy to do. You should not only read and study the Bible; you should read other books as well. A workman, he said, "needs not be ashamed." You need not be ashamed of rightly dividing the Word of truth. What the apostle was telling us is that proper Bible study will lead to approval from God. It will also build your faith and deepen your love for Christ as well as your passion for souls. If you are going to know the Bible inside out, it will take a lifetime. However, God will open the mind of your spiritual understanding. (**Psalm 119:18 and John 16:13**) True biblical knowledge and understanding comes from diligent effort and God's spirit working in you. God expects us to familiarize ourselves with His Word. Only then, by fully appreciating it, can we (1) act on it, and (2) be able to impart it to others. In Matthew 4 Jesus said, "Man shall not live by bread alone but by every word

> True biblical knowledge and understanding come from diligent effort and God's Spirit working in you.

that proceeded out of the mouth of God." **Psalm 119:105** says His Word is a lamp unto our feet and a light unto our path.

This is why Paul admonishes Timothy in **2 Timothy 3:15**, "And that from childhood you have known the holy scriptures, which are able to make you wise for salvation through faith which is in Christ Jesus." Verses 16-17 add: "All scripture is given by inspiration of God, and is profitable for doctrine, for reproof, for correction, for instruction in righteousness, that the man of God may be complete"—and don't miss this—"thoroughly equipped for every good work."

Notice that the Scripture is therefore an excellent instruction manual, providing a basis for doctrine, reproof, correction, and instruction so that you may be equipped for every good work. Therefore, using Scripture the witness is to lay the foundation and provide instruction regarding the way to salvation.

9.1 Rules for Answering Difficult Questions

When people ask difficult questions they are either searching for genuine answers or trying to refute what you have to say. In either case, the following rules apply:

9.2 Rule Number 1 (Be Honest)

When a person is seeking genuine answers, you will probably not find them too awkward to deal with. This is because you have already convinced them of their need of salvation or, if they are not yet fully persuaded they possess a genuine heart that is leaning toward the truth.

In either case the first rule is to be honest. Let honesty be your best policy. Whatever you do, do not attempt to answer questions for which you don't know the answers. Doing this makes you look dishonest and false, and that's the last impression you want to leave. If you don't know the answer, simply say so.

On the other hand, most of the people who are likely to pose difficult questions with intent to test your knowledge are likely to fall into one of the following categories:

1. People from different religious backgrounds
2. Atheists
3. Agnostics
4. Scientists
5. Those with no religious persuasion whatsoever.

Difficult questions can arise due to the diversity of peoples' backgrounds, and it may be hard to understand their motivation. But once again, honesty is always the best policy and will let them know you are a person of integrity. If you have no answer to their questions, you might want to say you will find out and get back with them. However, if you try to answer when you're unsure or have no clue and are found to be false, no one will take you seriously, and you have just lost your case.

In addition, you can also use that as an opportunity to invite them to your place of worship, for Bible study, or to meet your pastor for further clarification. Hopefully you have a good pastor, but you can say something like, "We have Bible study at our church on Wednesday nights at 7 p.m." (as the case may be) "Why don't you come along, to get the answers to your questions?"

9.3 Rule Number 2 (The burden of proof)

Some of the most common and yet difficult questions are about the existence of God, Evolution and the Creation, science, and other Bible subjects. If the question challenges the existence of God, the burden of proof belongs to the person asking the question.

What I'm saying here is that if someone challenges the existence of God it is his responsibility to prove there is no God, rather than your responsibility to prove there is. As quickly as you can, move the ball into their court. I will explain in greater detail how to do this in Chapter 10.

9.4 Rule Number 3 (Use Your Testimony)

It may come as a surprise to you when I suggest that you use your testimony when answering difficult questions. Your testimony may not actually answer the question, but it will shift the focus onto you and your personal experience with God.

In fact, in my opinion, one of the best methods of sharing the good news of salvation is with your testimony. Here is why it's so effective: People hate it when others point out their faults. And under most circumstances it's very hard to share regarding a person's need of a Savior without mentioning their sin.

But, when you share your testimony, it diverts the finger from pointing to them to focusing on you. Having said that, there is a catch—just any old testimony, won't do. It must be a testimony full of excitement telling of a recent divine encounter or a spectacular, life-changing but supernatural event that occurred in your life. I like to refer to it as a praise report. It should be just like sharing the excitement after receiving a brand new Mercedes Benz as a gift. Don't tell me you are not going to be calling family, friends, and neighbors with the most exciting news of your life and to invite them to come and share the occasion with you!

You really should be that excited about what God is doing in your life. **Psalm 19:7** says, "The testimony of the Lord is sure converting the soul, the testimony of the Lord is right enlightening the eyes, the testimony of the Lord is sure making wise the simple."

"The Holy Scripture is of much greater benefit to us than day or night, than the air we breathe, or the light of the sun. To restore man from his fallen state, the Word of God is necessary. The word translated "law" may be rendered doctrine, and may be understood to mean all that teaches us true religion. The whole is perfect; its tendency is to convert or turn the soul from sin and the world, to God and holiness. It shows our sinfulness and misery in departing from God, and the necessity of our return to him. This testimony is sure, to be fully depended on: the ignorant and unlearned believing what God is saying become wise unto salvation. It is a sure direction in the way of duty. It is a sure fountain of living comforts and a sure foundation of lasting hopes"

Perhaps right now you're saying, "I can't think of a thing God has done for me lately." Well, if that describes you it's probably because you aren't counting your blessings. Sometimes we only attach importance to the things we believe He *should give* to us and not to the things He wants us to have. For example, you may have prayed a long time for something important for you, such as a husband or a wife, and it hasn't happened yet. As a result, you may not be noticing the numerous blessings God is pouring out on your life and that of your family and friends. You must remember that your life is not so much about the physical. If you feel God has not done anything for you lately, it may be that you are not passionate enough about the spiritual aspect of your life to notice.

Another reason a testimony is powerful is that people are more likely to relate to real-life situations, especially if they are not generally receptive to the things of God.

9.3.1 A Good Testimony

Let me give you an idea of what I call a good testimony vs. a lazy person's testimony.

Depending on your background you may be familiar with what some churches used to call "testimony services." There you would often hear people mention part of a hymn or some other Christian cliché, such as "Praise the Lord! I'm saved, sanctified, Holy Ghost filled, water-baptized, and with Jesus on my mind, I am running for my life." Or "Jesus saves and He keeps and He satisfies, He's a wonderful friend of mine." That was the kind of testimony you would hear, especially from the older folks. In fact, I still hear people giving the same type of testimony thirty years later. In case you can't figure it out this is a lazy man's version of a testimony.

Here is an idea of a great testimony. I have a pastor friend from Singapore who talks about how he was an idol worshiper who had never even heard of Jesus until the Lord showed up in his bedroom to reveal Himself to him. Or, what about the testimony of the lady who had no food for her children? She filled a pot with water and turned on the flame under it then started praying. When the pot ran out of water she filled it again repeatedly, until finally a man rode up on a motorcycle, handed her a bag of groceries, and told her his wife was out of town, so he had no use for so much food. You may have had similar experiences when you did not know how you were going to make it through but God miraculously brought you through it. I could go on and on, but you get the picture. If you tell of incredible real life experiences it will come alive for the listener as nothing else can.

I can hear you argue that even then you will have skeptics. Should anyone challenge you by asking how you can be sure that it was God simply point them to the evidence. Check out the story told in **John, Chapter 9:2-25** when Jesus healed the blind man.

> Now as Jesus passed by, He saw a man who was blind from birth. And His disciples asked Him, saying, "Rabbi, who sinned, this man or his parents, that he was born blind?: Jesus answered, "Neither this man nor his parents sinned, but that the works of God should be revealed in him. I must work the works of Him who sent Me while it is day; the night is coming when no one can work. As long as I am in the world, I am the light of the world." When He had said these things, He spat on the ground and made clay with the saliva; and He anointed the eyes of the blind man with the clay. And He said to him, "Go, wash in the pool of Siloam" (which is translated 'sent'). So he went and washed, and came back seeing. Therefore the neighbors and those who previously had seen that he was blind said, "Is not this he who sat and begged?" Some said, "This is he." Others said, "He is like him." He said, "I am he." Therefore they said to him, "How were

your eyes opened?" He answered and said, "A Man called Jesus made clay and anointed my eyes and said to me, 'Go to the pool of Siloam and wash.' So I went and washed, and I received sight." Then they said to him, "Where is He?" He said, "I do not know." They brought him who formerly was blind to the Pharisees. Now it was a Sabbath when Jesus made the clay and opened his eyes. Then the Pharisees also asked him again how he had received his sight. He said to them, "He put clay on my eyes, and I washed, and I see." Therefore some of the Pharisees said, "This Man is not from God, because He does not keep the Sabbath." Others said, "How can a man who is a sinner do such signs?" And there was a division among them. They said to the blind man again, "What do you say about Him because He opened your eyes?" He said, "He is a prophet." But the Jews did not believe concerning him, that he had been blind and received his sight, until they called the parents of him who had received his sight. And they asked them, saying, "Is this your son, who you say was born blind? How then does he now see?" His parents answered and said, "We know that this is our son, and that he was born blind; but by what means he now sees we do not know, or who opened his eyes we do not know. He is of age; ask him. He will speak for himself." His parents said these things because they feared the Jews, for the Jews had agreed already that if anyone confessed that He was Christ, he would be put out of the synagogue. Therefore his parents said, "He is of age; ask him." So they again called the man who was blind, and said to him, "Give God the glory! We know that this Man is a sinner." He answered and said, "Whether He is a sinner or not I

> do not know. One thing I know: that though I was blind, now I see."

What an awesome testimony; in essence, it does not matter what your opinion is: all I know is once I was blind but now I can see. In other words, let the evidence of your testimony speak for itself.

9.4 Rule Number 3 (Avoid All Religious Conflicts)

Recently I was traveling on a flight from Kingston to Toronto, and as I normally did, I engaged the person sitting beside me. Initially, she was very defensive and inquisitive, wanting to know my religious affiliation. She only relaxed once she understood that I was not interested in bombarding her with my religious beliefs. This lady happens to be a Christian but had become weary of dealing with those who want to push their religious beliefs on her. By that she meant those who would argue that she was wrong for believing certain doctrines.

Whatever you do when witnessing, do not enter into debates or any form of heated or religious argument with anyone; it is not worth it and will leave a bad taste in the other person's mouth, completely negating your efforts. Winning an argument is not a kingdom principle. **2 Corinthians 10:5** tells us, "There is a spirit in us that seeks to exalt itself against the knowledge of God." This character trait leads to arguments and debates and most importantly, a need to be right at all costs. This is very self-centered and therefore does not bring glory to God.

Let's look at this in context, starting at verse 3:

> For though we walk in the flesh, we do not war according to the flesh. For the weapons of our warfare are not carnal, but mighty in God for the pulling down of strong-holds. Casting down arguments and every high thing that exalts itself against the knowledge of God. Bringing every

thought into captivity to the obedience of Christ and being ready to punish all disobedience when your obedience is fulfilled.

This passage teaches us that the war of the flesh includes strongholds, arguments, and every high thing that exalts itself against the knowledge of God. Those who want to argue that there is no God and that all spiritual things are mere myth are only exalting themselves against God.

It may be impossible to be able to avoid all battles, arguments, and debates, but we can learn to recognize when the battle is not of God and will not lead anyone to salvation. So why get involved in such spiritual and emotional conflicts? "Stand still and know that He is God, there's no need to fight, the battle is not yours, the battle is the Lord's."

Many of us waste copious amounts of time in such religious conflicts, which will result in nothing but grief. In conclusion, answering difficult questions can be avoided by simply being honest about whether or not you know the answer and by avoiding difficult questions altogether by shifting the burden of proof (especially where they are arguing that there is no God) and using your testimony where possible.

Chapter Checklist

In review, the rules include:

- The need to adopt a new lifestyle which should be reflected in the way you think and the way you speak.
- The need for honesty and integrity.
- It is not your responsibility to prove, such things as the existence of God; it is the non-believer's responsibility to prove that God does not exist.
- Your testimony is a great tool to use when witnessing,

------------------------------- Questions -----------------------------------

---

1. What kind of teaching was creeping into the church in Colossae?

---

2. What was the primary reason for this kind of teaching?

---

3. Who is the supreme and unseen witness?

---

4. What is the main function of the Holy Spirit?

---

5. What is the answer to every important question in life?

---

6. What was it Paul admonished Timothy not to do as a workman?

---

7. What lesson can we learn from the answer to question 6?

---

8. Complete the following Bible text: "All scripture is given by God for...)

---

9. What is the first rule for answering difficult questions?

---

10. Should someone try to lure you into a debate for example, regarding whether or not there is a God, how should you respond?

---

11. How can your testimony be used when answering difficult questions?

Personal Notes

SECTION 4

How to Witness to Different Groups of Individuals

Chapters 10 - 11

= CHAPTER TEN =

How to Witness To Different Groups of Individuals

If you are to master the art of personal evangelism, it will be necessary for you to know how to deal with different groups of people. The reason for this is, in order to have an amicable discussion you may need a different approach for each group.

In this chapter we will look at certain select groups, but the list is not exhaustive. We will consider the religious, the neighbor, those you know, those who are hurting, the atheist, the agnostic, and Muslims. This detailed background information will help you understand and relate to them more easily.

10.1 Witnessing to the Religious Person

Have you ever tried witnessing to a religious person? If you have, I am sure you know that they are unquestionably the most difficult people to reach with the gospel. Believe it or not, this is even more difficult with "religious Christians" for the want of a better word. But who am I referring to when I speak of religious Christians? A religious Christian can fall into a number of categories, for example:-

1. Those who were brought up in the church but have never made a personal commitment to follow Jesus. They know the Bible and can sometimes talk about it passionately. They also know about God but do not know Him personally.

2. Then there are those who classify themselves as, "good persons." We know, however, that no one has a right to make such a claim. Do you recall Jesus having to deal with this very issue? "Now as He was going out on the road, one came running, knelt before Him, and asked Him, 'Good Teacher, what shall I do that I may inherit eternal life?' So Jesus said to him, 'Why do you call Me good? No one is good but One, that is, God'" (**Mark 10:17**). Before I make my point, let me clarify this for you. I believe He was making the point that if the religious folks of His day did not believe He was God, how then could He be referred to as good since He was seen as an ordinary man? He may also have been saying that the man in question was a hypocrite because he did not accept Jesus for who He was. In other words, Jesus was simply pointing out the fact that no man can claim to be good. When a person believes he/she is good, it is not always easy to convince him/her otherwise. This group does not even recognize the need for a Savior.

3. Then there are those who are influenced along certain doctrinal lines. They believe that if you are not from their church, organization, and background, you are doomed. But we know from Scripture that Jesus teaches otherwise. As I have mentioned before, this is what is referred to as sectarianism, and we know that Jesus was not in agreement with this ideology. "Now John answered and said, 'Master, we saw someone casting out demons in Your name, and we forbade him because he does not follow with us.' But Jesus said to him, 'Do not forbid him, for he who is not against us is on our side'" (**Luke 9:49–50**).

4. Finally, there are those who are of other religious persuasions, such as Hindu, Muslim, etc.

In order to help you fully appreciate this concept of religion, let's look at another definition for clarity. The Merriam-Webster's defines the word religion as "relating to or devoted to religious belief, manifesting faithful devotion to an acknowledged ultimate reality or deity, scrupulously and consciously faithful."

This means that a religious belief is not necessarily based on facts or truth, but is simply based on a belief system, stuck in tradition. "That's what I've always believed." "My grandmother told me so." "That's what my pastor says." "That's what my holy book teaches." You get the picture.

When witnessing, it is necessary to know when you are speaking to a religious person. So how do you identify a religious person? That is simple: if the person does not have a Christian influence. For example, if the person is a Sikh, a Muslim, or a Hindu, etc, it may not be difficult to learn their religious persuasion. If, however, the person has a Christian influence, the whole question becomes a little more acute because they attend church and call upon the name of Jesus like most of us do. Having said that, if you know what you are looking for, a religious person could still be easily identified. One of the ways of spotting them is to listen to what they have to say. Most of them hold the doctrine of their church organization to be of more importance than the Bible, Christ and the body of Christ. They will not see you as part of God's kingdom if you do not attend their church. A religious Christian will almost always identify themselves by saying something like "I am a..." and go on to name their church or their religious organization.

The most effective way to witness to a religious person is to make sure that you do not get diverted from the issue of salvation. (See chapter 11 "A Journey down the Roman Road to Salvation.") You can easily be sidetracked into debates about such things as whose religion is right, under what name should you be baptized, which day to worship, etc. This will inevitably result in conflict—this is a pointless exercise. It will be far more productive to keep the conversation on biblical facts such as the miracle of the birth of Christ and the importance of the resurrection and so on. Whatever you do, keep it simple; remember, this is not an intellectual exercise. Your main aim is to bring the person or persons to the saving knowledge of Jesus Christ.

It cannot be overemphasized that we are saved by grace and grace alone, and not by trusting in our own righteousness and religious traditions.

I can guarantee that you will have some problems convincing the religious person to make changes in their belief system. As a result, it is of utmost importance that you *aim at the conscience*, rather than at the intellect. One writer suggests that one of the best ways of doing this is to take them through the Law of God (the commandments) to show that they are condemned despite their works. You may have seen "The Way of the Master" TV program, where Ray Comfort and Kirk Cameron go out on the streets asking people random questions including:

- Have you ever told a lie?
- Have you ever stolen anything from anyone?

This is a very practical way to get people to stop and think. I must admit that this is not my method of operation, however, if you are comfortable with it by all means go ahead and use it.

If they are open to the gospel and are truly interested in what God's Word says in reference to their church's teachings, they will listen to you. Once again, I would hope that you are at least involved in daily Bible study. Every born-again Christian should know the Word so that in the moment of need the Holy Spirit will bring back to memory what you need.

10.2 Witnessing to Those in Your Neighborhood

Those closest to us, including our families, friends, and neighbors are right up there with the religious people as the most difficult to witness to. Our neighbors are pretty much like family; we do not want to offend them unnecessarily because we have to live with them, and therefore we sometimes prefer to keep silent. The problem is, we cannot afford to have them living next door and never seize the opportunity to share the gospel of Christ with them. In that regard, I would remind you of **Mathew 5:13-16—**

> "You are the salt of the earth; but if the salt loses its flavor, how shall it be seasoned? It is then good for nothing but to be thrown out and trampled underfoot by men. You are the light of the world. A city that is set on a hill cannot be hidden. Nor do they light a lamp and put it under a basket, but on a lamp stand, and it gives light to all who are in the house. Let your light so shine before men, that they may see your good works and glorify your Father in heaven."

One Bible commentary explained it this way: "You are the salt of the earth. Mankind, lying in ignorance and wickedness, were as a vast heap, ready to putrefy; but Christ sent forth his disciples, by their lives and doctrines to season it with knowledge and grace. If they are not such as they should be, they are as salt that has lost its savor. If a man can take up the profession of Christ, and yet remain graceless, no other doctrine, no other means, can make him profitable. Our light must shine, by doing such good works as men may see. What is between God and our souls, must be kept to ourselves; but that which is of itself open to the sight of men, we must study to make suitable to our profession, and praiseworthy. We must aim at the glory of God." Matthew Henry Commentary.

It means, therefore, that we need to abound in good works towards men, but especially to our neighbors. The Bible lets us know that this is a legitimate means of evangelism. According to **1 Peter 2:15**, it is God's will that "with well doing you may put to silence the ignorance of foolish men."

The bottom line is, sinners and in particularly your neighbors, may disagree with what you believe, but they will not be able to argue against your good works.

This is why it's so vital to allow your actions to speak, especially by always showing warm acknowledgement and expressing an interest in their wellbeing. I used to like planting vegetables during the summer months, and it was my pleasure to share them with my neighbors at harvest times. If your neighbor is elderly, why not offer to mow the lawn or clean the windows? Offer to pick up groceries if you are going to the market. Be complimentary when appropriate, and invite them for family occasions such as barbecues and other special events.

10.3 Witnessing to People You Know

As with witnessing to your neighbors, it is always much easier to witness to strangers than to those you know. But the following suggestions can be helpful:

10.3.1 Use Praise Reports

In the previous chapter when we discussed how to answer difficult questions, I told you your testimony could be used to great effect. That suggestion will also be applicable here.

Praise reports are one of the most powerful means of communicating the message of salvation to the people you know, because a testimony speaks for itself. When testifying, you are not directly telling anyone about your religious belief, and it is far less imposing. Above all, the evidence of such testimonies is undeniable. Remember, do not worry about the end result; leave that to God.

When giving your testimony, be sure to let honesty and integrity be your partners; in other words, be very truthful and humble. This is imperative because one of the main reasons it is difficult to witness to those you know is because they see your life. They know your weaknesses and your faults and will not hesitate to point them out should you operate out of a spirit of self-righteousness.

10.3.2 Give Them a Point of Reference

Suppose you want to share the gospel with a work colleague or a fellow student—someone you have known for a long time but have never seriously engaged in a spiritual conversation. Maybe for you, these are people who do not understand and appreciate the seriousness of your commitment to God. Maybe the truth is that you were not that committed but now you are and feel you must reach them. I suggest that you arrive at work on Monday morning with the goal of setting a new precedent. In a very excitable tone tell them, "I went to church yesterday," then tell them how it changed your life and that you have decided to make some changes. Then begin by making this a habit at every opportunity. Notice, you are not telling anyone about religion. You are merely sharing what God is doing in your life. This method works every time.

In doing this you are breaking the stronghold that has hindered your witness. From then on, you will want to emphasize how much you've changed by excluding yourself from those things you should not do. These may include: gossip, idle talk, or drinking and partying—you get the picture. If you do not follow through in this area, I guarantee that they will see you as a hypocrite. But now you have given them a point of reference from which to judge you, i.e., that Monday morning. The chances are, they may not take you seriously to begin with, but over time they will see evidence of change and cease to judge you based on your past behavior.

10.3.3 Use the First Person Approach

When witnessing to those who know our faults it's best to use a first person approach, saying something like: "Though I have attended church for ten years, I did not truly appreciate the power of God to change lives." Or if they are unbelievers, you might say, "I've attended church for some time but until now I never realized the Bible is the final authority regarding my eternal destiny." This is likely to induce one of two responses: First, it may arouse curiosity, or it will inevitably open up a floodgate of questions. Either way, it will serve as your opportunity to share the gospel.

Once again, I cannot overemphasize the importance of honesty. It is important that you be quick to admit faults and mistakes, etc. People are not stupid; they know you are human and subject to error. You will gain more respect being honest than from pretending to be perfect when it's clearly not so.

10.4 Witnessing to Those who are Hurting

There's a good chance that your greatest challenge will be to witness to those who are hurting. Why? Because they require special care and understanding. It will take all your resources to be effective and to exercise good judgment.

For example, this week the world has turned its attention to the recent earthquake in Haiti. Many of us are grieved in our spirits as we imagine the trauma that countless numbers of people must be experiencing when they realize their loved ones and friends are missing. Think about it—when your mother cannot be found and is presumed buried alive under a mound of rubble—when your toddler is shaken from your arms never to be seen again. How do you impart comfort to those in deep suffering? Even the hard-hearted and closed-minded begin to take stock during trying times like these.

At such times some will question the very existence of a sovereign God. Others will point an accusing finger toward the sin of the victims as if they deserved such a fate.

Not only that but, what do you say to the lady whose husband has just walked out on their ten-year marriage for a younger woman? What do you say to a person facing bereavement? How do you witness to the hurting? In those situations you must be very sensitive to the immediate need of the one who is suffering. Yet at the same time we cannot ignore the need for that person's salvation. I would recommend here that you gently share with them, allowing your conversation to revolve around the amazing love of God. You need to reassure them that God longs to comfort them in their time of need. It may take a little practice on your part in order to deal with both simultaneously. Having said that, it is an area with which we should all become proficient at if we want to win the lost for Christ.

> You must be very sensitive to the immediate need of the person who is going through suffering while showing them that God loves them.

A few years ago, I was witnessing to a young English lady who obviously did not come from a Christian background. She was grieving the recent loss of her brother. Evidently hurting from the experience, she asked me, "How can I believe in a God who caused my brother to die?" When people are grieving, they experience a wide range of emotions simultaneously including denial, shock, anger, resentment, bitterness, and perhaps even revenge. Some will even harbor bitterness toward God. How then do you witness to such a person? What would you think their reaction would be if you were to approach them talking about sin, righteousness, and judgment?

Tell the person you are sorry for their loss. Again make sure to show genuine sensitivity. But you must waste no time in turning to the serious issue at hand—the person's salvation. (This should be done with love and compassion.) As in the example above, unless the person is a Christian, stay clear of any talk about whether or not the person who died went to heaven or hell by saying that God is good and that He will do that which is right on the Day of Judgment.

For someone who is suffering bereavement, your line of conversation should go something like, "Whenever we as human beings are confronted with the issue of death, it can often make us think about God, and our own eternal salvation."

If, during your deliberation you said anything to offend, be very quick to apologize and change the subject, but more than likely, you will find that by talking about their personal salvation, it will be like a complete subject change, and hopefully they will not find you too offensive.

If you perceive that the individual is bitter toward God and that is hindering him/her from opening up his/her heart, calmly let him/her know that like him/her, "Many people have suffered terrible losses and they have let that suffering bring them to the cross, and consequently to everlasting life in Christ Jesus." Perhaps you could share this analogy: If you are drowning and someone offers to save you, don't let the fact that you don't like them prevent you from accepting their help. God promises to save us in times of trouble so we should encourage them to trust in God and allow Him to rescue them, in their distress.

Very few people in the world can claim to have escaped suffering. Reports have shown that 200,000 people were murdered in the USA in the 1990s, and recently we have seen an increase in other natural disasters such as tsunamis, hurricanes, and volcanoes that have wrought havoc in the lives of many. This leaves a large number of people around the world who point an accusing finger at God. Most expect Him to immediately fix those problems they consider the most serious or else they curse Him to His face. However, God wants to deal with the most urgent issue of sin and grant them eternal life through Jesus Christ. Therefore, if as Christians we care about the will of God and the eternal welfare of those to whom we are speaking, we must deal with the issue of their soul even though they are in emotional pain.

10.5 Witnessing to Atheists

From a personal perspective augmented by scriptures, I do not believe there is any such person as an atheist. *Webster's Dictionary* describes an atheist as someone "not believing in the existence of God or any other deity," but there is only one way to describe such a person who said there is no God— "a fool." **Psalm 14:1** tells us: "The fool has said in his heart 'there is no God'; they are corrupt, they have done abominable works, there is none who does good."

Psalm 19 says,

> The heavens declare the glory of God and the firmament shows His handiwork. Day unto day utters speech, and night unto night reveals knowledge. There is no speech or language where their voice is not heard. Their line has gone out through all the earth and their words to the end of the worlds. In them he has set a tabernacle for the sun, which is like a bridegroom coming out of his chamber. And rejoices like a strong man to run a race. Its rising is from one end of heaven. And its circuit to the other end; and there is nothing hidden from its heat." Then He said this: "The law of the Lord is perfect, converting the soul; the testimony of the Lord is sure, making wise the simple; The statutes of the Lord are right, rejoicing the heart; The commandments of the Lord are pure, enlightening the eyes; the fear of the Lord is clean, enduring forever; the judgment of the Lord is true and righteous altogether. More to be desired are they than gold, yea, than much fine gold; sweeter also than honey and the honey comb.

Listen to verse 11:

> "Moreover by them your servant is warned, and in keeping them, there is great reward. Who can understand His errors? Cleanse me from secret faults. Keep back your servant from presumptuous sins; Let them not have dominion over me. Then I shall be blameless. And I shall be innocent of great transgression."

Here the Scripture is saying that the heavens declare God's glory and also proclaim His wisdom, His power, and His goodness. But listen to this, so that all ungodly men are left without excuse. Paul picks up the story in **Romans 1: 18-32** when he tells us:

> "For the wrath of God is revealed from heaven against all ungodliness and unrighteousness of men, who suppress the truth in unrighteousness, because what may be known of God is manifest in them, for God has shown it to them. For since the creation of the world his invisible attributes are clearly seen, being understood by the things that are made, even His eternal power and Godhead, so that they are without excuse. Because although they knew God, they did not glorify Him as God, nor were thankful, but became futile in their thoughts, and their foolish hearts were darkened. Professing to be wise they became fools, and changed the glory of the incorruptible God into an image made like corruptible man, and birds and four footed animals and creeping things. Therefore God also gave them up to uncleanness, in the lust of their hearts, to dishonor their bodies among themselves, who exchange the truth of God into a lie, and worship and serve the creature rather than the creator, who is blessed forever,

> amen. For this reason God gave them up to vile passions. For even their women exchange the natural use for what is against nature. Likewise also the men, leaving the natural use of the woman, burned in their lusts for one another, men with men committing what is shameful, and receiving in themselves the penalty of their error which was due. And even as they did not like to retain God in their knowledge, God gave them over to a debased mind, to do the things which are not fitting; being filled with all unrighteousness, sexual immorality, wickedness, covetousness, maliciousness; full of envy, murder, strife, deceit, evil-mindedness; they are whisperers, backbiters, haters of God, violent, proud, boasters, inventers of evil things, disobedient to parents, undiscerning, unworthiness, unloving, unforgiving, unmerciful; Who knowing the righteous judgment of God, that those who practice such things are deserving of death, nor only do the same but also approve of those who practice them."

Here the apostle Paul clearly states that all mankind needs salvation, in that we cannot obtain the favor of God or escape His wrath by our own works or believing whatever we please. The sinfulness of man is simply described as ungodliness "against the law of the first table" and "unrighteousness against those of the second," which make reference to the Old and the New Testament Scriptures. Just because someone says they do not believe in God, it does not mean that God will get up and roll up the heavens like a scroll and pack it away saying, "I can't be bothered." In other words, no matter what someone believes, it will not cause heaven to cease, or cause the order of heaven to be disrupted.

Here Paul was emphasizing that their sin was in holding the truth in unrighteousness, doing what they knew to be wrong, while omitting what they knew to be right. He eliminated ignorance as an excuse for sin. "Therefore you are without excuse" (Romans 2:1). They are without excuse because our Creator's invisible power and Godhead are so clearly shown in the works of His hand that even those who classify themselves as atheists, agnostics, idol worshippers, and the wicked are left with no excuse. Paul is saying that they foolishly followed idolatry, and rational creatures changed the worship of the glorious creator to that of brutes, reptiles, and senseless images. They wandered from God until all traces of true godliness were lost.

Amid the depravity of such irreligious concepts, the Word of the Lord was revealed. "Light was come into the world but men loved darkness rather than light (**John 3:19**)."

Psalm 19 brings us this revelation so that we can all grasp the truth—that no man can claim to be ignorant of God because His glory is demonstrated everywhere we look. One doesn't have to be a genius to see evidence of a divine Creator who is eternal, intelligent and powerful. The changing from day to night, for example, is absolute proof of the power of God that simply cannot be denied.

In other words there are no atheists; rather these are people who allow their foolish hearts to deceive them. Atheism is the "ultimate intellectual suicide." It is probably true that Christians possess a faith that makes no logical sense. (The operative word here is *logical.*) But that's okay because logic is science and God cannot be perceived logically or otherwise, scientifically.

However, when witnessing to so-called atheists, you must remember to put the burden of proof on them—that it is their responsibility to prove there is no God, and not for you to prove there is. At no time will I tell the atheist in so many words that this is my position; however, in an unassuming way, I will immediately encourage that person to prove it.

10.5.1 A Practical Example

A few years ago, I walked into a doctor's office full of enthusiasm and a burning desire to share the gospel. I can't recall how I started the conversation, but I can remember the doctor telling me, he did not believe in God, and that he only believed in science. The Lord spoke to me immediately and I said to him, "Sir, let's talk about science for a moment." Notice that at that point I was not talking about Jesus or anything of any religious nature. I was actually talking to him about science, the very thing he said he believed in. First I asked him to agree with me that Albert Einstein is considered to be the greatest scientist of our time. Notice again what I was doing: I was playing ball on his turf, getting him to agree with me. At that point I drew his attention to a statement made by Albert Einstein in which he said, "Logic will take you from A – B but imagination will take you anywhere." I proceeded to remind him that science is based on logical assumptions and that Einstein agreed that even science has its limitations. Let me just interject here to pre-empt what you may be thinking. You may be thinking that you know nothing about Albert Einstein or his quotations. Well, you do now.

> Logic will take you from A – B, but imagination will take you anywhere." **Albert Einstein**

The question then is, what is imagination? Here is the definition of imagination: "The faculty or action of producing mental images of what is not present." In other words, it allows you to see the unseen. Well, that is the exact definition of faith: "Faith is a strong and unshakable belief in something without proof,"—that is, without scientific evidence. Isn't it then obvious that Albert Einstein is by his own admission saying that there is more to life than that which can be proven by science?

Right then the Lord spoke to me and I asked him, "Sir, when you leave your office this evening, how can you apply science to get you home? Can you apply science to prevent a vehicle from running off the road and knocking you over on the sidewalk?" I don't know where that analogy came from, but I could tell he was dumbfounded because I had just proven to him that (1) whatever he said he believed in was a fallacy, and (2) it could not be relied upon. Notice that I did not directly reintroduce the subject of religion or say anything else offensive. In fact, I said all these things in a warm and friendly way.

In the end, once he said he only believed in science, I merely set out to prove that what he said he believed was a fallacy and left him to make up his own mind. Okay, I know that kind of approach takes a lot of experience, but here is what you can do. You can ask the person to tell you what their opinion is based on. If they say it's based on science, then ask for proof. If they say it's based on their own opinion, ask them to explain why you should rely on their opinion. I guarantee they will tie themselves up in the process. Again, what you are doing here is asking them to defend their case.

Here is one last illustration. Recently I was having a conversation with an elderly man at my local gym. He was telling me that he was not well and I had planned to pray for him, but first I asked if he believed in God. He responded by saying that we Christians were brainwashed, so I asked him to explain how he concluded that I was brainwashed about the existence of God and indeed he could not. I asked whether that was his own opinion or whether it was something he had read, and still he had no answer. Can you see how this approach works? If he had said the Bible was written by mere men then I would have wanted to know why his book's author was any more valid than those who wrote the Bible. On the other hand, if he was merely sharing his own opinion then I would ask why that should hold any more weight than the opinions of the other seven billion people on the planet. Can you see what happened here? I have put him on the defensive, forcing him to prove his point, rather than forcing me to prove mine.

10.6 Witnessing to Agnostics

An agnostic is a person who believes that it is impossible to know whether there is a supreme being or God. In other words, the agnostic is skeptical about the existence of God. But while he is doubtful, he does not profess true atheism.

In simple terms an agnostic claims to have no knowledge of the existence of God. In fact, the term "agnostic" literally means "no knowledge." They do not have a commonly accepted set of views, but rather a variety of views including:

One of the two most common forms is called Weak Agnosticism. While this view believes that God is unknown, it accepts the fact that God may be known, and some people may possibly know Him. The second form, Strong Agnosticism, maintains that God is unknowable, and that He cannot be known.

Limited agnosticism says that God is partially unknown because of our finite minds. This view holds that we can know some things about God, but we cannot know everything. Unlimited agnosticism claims that God is completely unknowable. That is, that it's impossible to truly know anything about God.

Agnostic views stem from views regarding the ability to know reality. These views of reality were most strongly advocated by David Hume and Immanuel Kant. David Hume was technically a skeptic, but his views led to agnosticism. One of his foremost beliefs was that everything we experience is totally separate and unconnected. The cause-and-effect relationships that we observe can never really be known with any certainty. Instead, Hume thought, causal relationships are based solely on observation, and we see causality as we link events that occur together.

Immanuel Kant was greatly influenced by the ideas of Hume. Kant held that knowledge is provided by experience through the senses. He concluded that we can never know actual reality as it truly is if we are dependent on our senses. We can only know something as we experience it in ourselves. Since everyone experiences the same event differently, we can never know the event as it actually happened outside of ourselves.

The views of Hume and Kant have had a powerful impact on peoples' views about God. What this is saying is, if you cannot know reality as it actually is, then you really can't even know events, as they are independent of our senses. Also, you can't really know the true causes of any given event if everything is unconnected. Interestingly enough, however, even with this in mind, the agnostic claims he actually does know the possible origin of the universe.

10.6.1 A Practical Illustration

Let me give you a practical example of how I deal with the agnostics. It was about three years ago when I was in the South East area of London, UK. It was a Sunday night and I was on my way home from church when I stopped to get something to eat. Somehow I got into a conversation in which I was sharing the gospel with four obviously highly-educated English guys. The leader in the group started out by telling me that he did not believe in a God but that he believed in an energy.

Well, I perceived that this was leading to the big bang theory, and therefore I picked up the story. I started by asking him a question seemingly unrelated on the surface. "Do you know that there are more than 50 billion galaxies and that in each galaxy there are billions of stars?" I asked him. Then I went on to tell him that these galaxies were spinning round and round, and then I introduced the concept of God. I told him that God sits on the circle of the earth and so on **(Isaiah 40:22).** Can you see what I was doing? I was painting a picture of (1) the wonder of this great universe in which we live together with God's incredible creativity and order. And (2) that explosions cannot create such order. I believe my message got home because within half an hour, one of them asked me, "Where is your church and where are you preaching next?"

I know many of you may be thinking that you do not have that natural propensity to think like that and neither do you possess that kind of knowledge. Well, as I have said on previous occasions, you do not really need knowledge to witness but it does help, so you must be a "student for life." Many of you do not take notepads and pens to church. You must take notes, because it helps. Having said that, the chances are that you may not have to face these situations in your lifetime and even if you did and failed, it's not the end of your world. The most important thing to remember is that we witness by serving others with a kind and joyful spirit, and that should be your primary goal.

10.7 Witnessing to Muslims

Perhaps you have heard the name "Muslim" but have no idea what it means or who they are.

Some Background Information

Islam is the world's second largest religion, with a following of approximately 1.3 billion people called Muslims.

Muslims can be found across the entire globe. And though they can be found in North and South America, the Caribbean, and Western Europe, they are mostly found in Africa, the Middle East, and Asia. According to Wikipedia, "Their most predominant homeland lies in the area commonly known as the 10/40 window" (between 10 degrees latitudinal north and 40 degrees latitudinal north ranging from the eastern side of North Africa to the western side of Asia). About 60% of Muslims are Asians. The regional breakdown of Muslims in the rest of the world is as follows: Arabs 22%, Sub-Sahara Africans 12%; Eastern Europe 5%, and the rest are scattered throughout the world.

Islam was founded in 610 A.D. by a man named Mohammed. During his time, people were worshipping multiple gods. The concept of worshipping many gods is known as polytheism. During one of Mohammed's trips as a trader, he claimed to have had a dream given to him by a being he perceived to be an angel who told him, "There is only one God, and his name is Allah. Worship him."

Just like the Christians who have the Bible and the Jews who have the Torah, the Muslims have the Quran. The Muslims believe that the Quran was dictated to Mohammed by God through the angel Gabriel. Muslims are also told in the Quran to read three other holy books: The Torah (which are the first five books of the Old Testament), the Zabur (which are the psalms of David), and the Injeel (the gospel of Christ). Just as Christians gather on Saturdays and Sundays, the Muslims gather in mosques on Fridays all around the world. They pray with their face towards Mecca, the birthplace of Islam where Mohammed is said to have had his vision.

There are seven fundamental beliefs of the Islamic faith that every Muslim must accept as part of their religion (the Emanul Mufassil or faith listed in details). As part of their religious training every Muslim must learn this formula.

1. "Belief in God, (who in Arabic, is named Allah")
2. "Belief in the angels (both good and bad)"
3. "Belief in the revealed books of God"
4. "Belief in God's many prophets (including Adam, Abraham, Moses, David, and others Christians and Jews are familiar with)"
5. "Accepting that there will be a last day"
6. "Belief in the divine measurement of human affairs"
7. "Belief in life after death"

Muslims also believe in Satan and the Day of Judgment, on which God will send people to either hell or heaven. They also believe that Ishmael (the father of the Arab world, and son of Abraham and Hagar the bondwoman), and not Isaac, received the promise from God through Abraham; this explains why Arab Muslims feel that their claim to the Holy Land is their God-given right.

Despite the fact that both Christianity and Islam share some terminology and even some theological concepts (including monotheism which means there is only one God), Islam is fundamentally different from Christianity in that, Islam is a works-based religion. Islam teaches that if God wants to forgive sins, He simply says it is forgiven, whereas in Christianity, the forgiveness of sin is based on salvation by grace through faith as a result of the shed blood of Christ. In other words, Christianity recognizes the necessity for the shedding of blood for the forgiveness of sin. **(See Hebrews 9:22.)**

All Muslims believe Jesus was born of a virgin and that He was a great prophet, but they believe He was only a prophet, rather than a deity. They believe that He was sent from God to help people obey God. Islam claimed that as a baby—Jesus spoke, healed the sick, and raised the dead. The Quran refers to Jesus as the breath of God, the spirit of God, the life of God, and the word of God. Muslims do not think Jesus died on a cross. They believe that right before He was to be killed, God took Him up to heaven and someone else, probably Judas, replaced Him on the cross. They believe Jesus will return to earth again, but they trust He will return to usher in the final judgment from God and confirm that Islam is the true and final religion for all mankind.

What Do Muslims Believe Saves Them?

Islam requires that its followers earn their way to heaven by performing the five pillars of the faith, as follows.

1. Say the confession of faith. A Muslim must confess, "There is no God but Allah and Mohammed is the prophet of God."
2. Pray. Muslims are supposed to pray five times a day: shortly before sunrise, mid-morning, noon, mid-afternoon, and after sunset.
3. Give alms. Muslims are to give about 5.5% of their wealth.
4. Fast during Ramadan. For one lunar month, from sunrise to sunset, Muslims are not to allow anything to pass down their throats (theoretically speaking, good Muslims do not allow even the saliva to pass down; instead they spit it out). Then from sunset to sunrise, they are permitted to eat as little or as much as they want. This is their way of developing discipline and relating to the poor. (Travelers, young children, and pregnant or nursing mothers do not need to keep the fast.)
5. Make pilgrimages to Mecca. Every Muslim who is financially able is supposed to travel to the birthplace of Islam once in his lifetime.

Do Muslims Have Any Guarantee of Salvation?

Muslims do not have any guarantee that they are saved. They believe that all their works will be accounted for and that on Judgment Day, if their bad work outweighs their good work, they will go to hell. But if their good works outweigh the bad, they will probably go to heaven. They believe that, "(Since God is all-powerful; He will do with us whatever He pleases, even if we have been very righteous. They hope God won't be having a bad day on judgment.)" A third possibility is that they could go to hell and burn their sins off for a while and then be allowed into heaven. The only way Muslims can be guaranteed a place in heaven is through "jihad." Although it is often translated as "holy war," jihad actually means exerting force for God. This could mean anything from writing a book about Islam or by sharing their faith to bring others to Islam or by physically fighting for the cause of Islam. If a Muslim dies in jihad, he is guaranteed a place in heaven.

Is there Any Variation in Islam?

Believe it or not, Islam varies greatly around the world. Despite the fact that Muslims go to great lengths to describe themselves as members of the brotherhood of "one religion," the Islam practiced in, say Africa—is far different from that which is practiced in Saudi Arabia, which is also different for that which is practiced in Iran, or Morocco. In fact, there are 72 different sects in Islam (as in denominations).

What Is the Difference between Shiite and Sunni Islam?

No doubt you have heard the terms "Shiite" and "Sunni", the two major sects in Islam. The fundamental difference between these two sects is that they disagree about the legitimate successors of Mohammed. About 85 percent of all Muslims are Sunni and only 10 percent are Shiite. (The remaining 5 percent are affiliated to other minor sects.)

How Do They View Christianity?

Most Muslims believe Christians believe in three gods: God the Father, God the Son, and God the Mother (Mary). They believe that Christians and Jews have changed the Bible; therefore, although the Quran acknowledges the Gospel of Christ, the Torah of Moses, and the Psalms of David, they believe the existing copies cannot be trusted. As a result they believe that all of these holy books are superseded by the Quran.

Why Is It So Hard to Lead Muslims to Christ?

It is hard to help Muslims come to Christ because of the factors that tie Muslims to their religion, for example:-

1. Culture - Probably the most fundamental factor that ties Muslims to their religion is their culture. Usually there is about 10% theological and 90% cultural. A few years ago, I worked alongside a Muslim lawyer and when our conversation turned to religion, he simply stated religion was an accident of birth. This is to say if I were born in Pakistan, there is a high chance that I would have been a Muslim as well.

2. Community – It is pertinent to Muslims to fit into a larger group of people in order to feel secure and to "belong." This could be an extended family, or a network of friends. This community is called an "umma" and it provides tremendous safety and security. If they ever lose their job, it's no problem! Their community will help them out until they find another job. When Muslims are confronted with the claims of Christ, they may know it to be truth, but they are much more worried about leaving their community. Some time ago, I visited a shop in Hammersmith, London, UK. One of the fellows said something about God, and inasmuch as he was from the Asian community, I asked him if he was a Christian. Placing his finger across his lips, he said, "Shh...,

> I am Muslim but I know what I believe when I go home." Apparently one of his parents was a believer and he knew the truth. But because many other Muslims worked there he did not want to risk that they would learn of his belief in Christ. Although I was glad to know he was a believer in Christ I warned him about the danger of denying Christ. The point is, he was concerned about being ostracized by his community.

Muslims who want to turn to Christ feel a strong need to find a community of Christians where they can belong, before they will accept the truth. The problem is, in most Muslim areas, there are no acceptable Christian communities, which makes it very difficult for Muslims to follow Christ.

Are Muslims Coming to Know Christ?

Christ is known to the Muslim community as "Isa al Masih." Most of them will just say "Isa" for short. The answer as to whether Muslims are coming to Christ is a resounding yes! It has been reported that since 1970, many more Muslims have come to know Jesus than at any other time in history.

One of the factors fostering the growth of the church within the Muslim communities is the fact that some converted Muslims worship Jesus in ways that more closely resemble their own culture. For instance, rather than calling their building a church they call it a mosque. They also pray five times a day as Muslims do. They may be attired differently than Western Christians and may follow the tradition of the washing of the feet before prayers. A follower of Jesus in such cultures may be indistinguishable to Western eyes. I hope that we in the Western world are rational enough to appreciate and respect this uniqueness of expression and worship of our Savior. The worship of Jesus transcends racial and cultural boundaries.

If you come across Muslims and want to share the gospel with them in an amicable way you must use a great deal of wisdom.

A Practical Illustration

A few years ago I was working alongside a colleague from Pakistan, (not the one mentioned earlier); we were both accountants, which provided a platform for mutual respect. As you can imagine, our conversation would, from time to time, turn to religion. In order to avoid any form of animosity between us, here is how I dealt with the matter.

I laid the foundation for the conversation by pointing out that anyone who has a desire to live godly should seek for truth. I put this in a way so that I could induce a response. In other words, I asked for his approval. Can you see how effective this can be? It was, in reality, a set up, because, had he rejected the idea, the conversation would have come to a premature end. However, he was an intelligent man so he expressed his agreement with me on that issue.

> Many people believe that truth is relative, but we know that truth is absolute. Not only that, but the Bible says, "You shall know the truth and the truth shall make you free."

The good news is that I soon had him in my corner so we could have a rational conversation. Regarding truth, many people believe that truth is relative, but we know that truth is absolute. And not only that, the Bible says: "You shall know the truth and the truth shall make you free." We also know that "I am" (Jesus) is "the way the truth and the life," no man comes to the father but by Him (Jesus.) So this will, by no means become a clash of religious ideologies. It has to do with finding the truth and living by it. I was pleasantly surprised when this man told me that Jesus is coming back to earth again. When I asked him why Mohammed was not coming back, he replied, "Because Mohammed is dead." I rest my case; I do not serve a dead God. Well, at the end of the conversation, fully persuaded, my colleague said, "I am going to get a Bible and read it from beginning to end."

My friends, it is not difficult to communicate the gospel to anyone. Remember, Jesus promised that when you go, you don't need to take anything with you because He will provide what you need at the moment you need it, including the words to say.

Notice that at no time have I argued whose religion is right. In fact, one of us often feels the need to dig deeper, to know more. Just keep it simple—it works every time.

Chapter Checklist

In review:

- Whatever you do, be courteous and loving at all times.
- Show a personal interest and remember to allow them to speak, i.e., let them articulate their views.
- It is helpful to understand their basic beliefs as set out in this chapter, but you may also want to investigate further.
- With regard to Muslims you must be willing to examine and cross-reference the Quran with respect to their beliefs.
- It is a big plus to know that the Quran says; things like Jesus is coming back again, the virgin birth, etc.
- Make sure you are aware of how the Quran refers to Christ—as the breath of God, the Spirit of God and the life of God.
- Stick to the doctrine of the Christian faith but also be sure to take time out to answer all genuine questions. I must emphasize again the need to be honest and say so if you don't know the answer.
- It is imperative that you place emphasis on the importance of Jesus in the process of salvation.
- Make it clear that because of Jesus, His death on the cross, and the resurrection from the dead, one may have the full assurance of salvation as set out in **1 John 5:13.**
- Clearly and coherently point out the plan of salvation, particularly that salvation is a gift and cannot be earned. See Chapter 11.
- Pray for the leading of the Holy Spirit, during your time of witness. Depend on the Spirit to provide you with wisdom and grace.

- Most importantly, you must be willing to become a friend; in other words, let the beauty and the love of Jesus shine through you in a magnificent way. Remember, "It's not what you say but how you say it."

--------------------------------- Questions: ---------------------------------

1. Name four reasons why it is difficult to witness to a religious Christian.

2. Jesus believed in Sectarianism. True/False

3. What scripture given in Like 10 proved that Jesus does not believe in sectarianism?

4. What will be the most likely result if you get sidetracked into debates?

5. When witnessing to a religious person, what should be your aim?

6. What is the best way to witness to people you know?

7. What are the other two ways given to witness to people you know?

---

8. What is the most important tool for witnessing to the hurting?

---

9. When witnessing to someone who is hurting, it is okay to ignore the salvation of their soul. True/False

---

10. On whom is the burden of proof when witnessing to an atheist or agnostic?

---

11. Who founded the Islamic faith?

---

12. What is the name of the Islamic holy book?

---

13. Name three other holy books Muslims are supposed to read.

---

14. Name five things Muslims think about Jesus.

15. How do Muslims think they are saved?

16. Do Muslims have any guarantee of salvation?

Personal Notes

= CHAPTER ELEVEN =

A Journey down the Roman Road to Salvation

It would be an injustice to complete a piece of work such as this without taking you down the Roman Road to salvation because the Book of Romans provides a simple yet profound explanation of the process of salvation. For example, Romans tells us:

a. Why everyone needs salvation!
b. How God made the provision for salvation!
c. How we can receive that salvation
d. The benefits of obtaining salvation

It is important that you study this carefully because if you do not know anything else you will need to know how to explain why everyone needs salvation. You may also be required to help your new prospect accept Christ as Lord and Savior.

This will be extremely pertinent when witnessing to those from other religions, and unbelievers, but it may be even more potent when witnessing to religious Christians. Many of these people believe that they do not need salvation, because they are good people. They will tell you of the good deeds they have done and that they have not hurt anybody, etc. No doubt you have come across people like that. That is why we must place strong emphasis on the truth that no one can earn their salvation by good works.

Let's go with the apostle Paul as he addresses these issues with the Romans.

The first question we must address is: why does everyone need salvation? **Romans 3:23** has the answer: "For all have sinned, and fall short of the glory of God." This is indeed your first port of call. Should someone ask you why they need salvation, your answer should be, because we all have sinned, we all have done wrong and displeased God no matter how good we may consider ourselves to be. And just in case someone thinks they have no sin, Paul explains in **Romans 3:10–18,**

> "As it is written: There is none righteous, no, not one. There is none who understands; there is none who seeks after God. They have all turned aside; they have together become unprofitable. There is none who does good, no, not one. Their throat is an open tomb. With their tongues they have practiced deceit; the poison of asps is under their lips; whose mouth is full of cursing and bitterness. Their feet are swift to shed blood; destruction and misery are in their ways. And the way of peace they have not known. There is no fear of God before their eyes."

So clearly we all have sinned and fallen short of God's glory.

Thank God Paul did not just expose us to the fact that we all have sinned without letting us know of the consequences. The second thing you must know is that there is a penalty for the sins we have committed. Romans 6:23 tells us, "For the wages of sin is death; but the gift of God is eternal life in Jesus Christ our Lord." There is a heavy price to be paid for sin and that is death and eternity in hell. Death and hell are the result of sin, and no one is exempt.

Paul then went on to say that, in spite of our sin, God made provision for our escape. Look at the second part of **Romans 6:23:** "But the gift of God is eternal life through Jesus Christ our Lord." Hallelujah, thank God he has not left us to die in our sins. Paul did not stop there, because in **Romans 5:8** he tells us how God did it. "But God demonstrates His own love toward us, in that while we were still sinners, Christ died for us." Many people will tell you that all religions lead to God, but that is not the case. There is no remission for sins, no forgiveness, apart from the death of Christ on the cross. Why? Because Jesus, the perfect Lamb of God, had to die in our stead to pay the price to redeem us back to God. Notice that the apostle did not just give us information about the consequences of sin and the gift of God, but he also told us how to obtain salvation. This can be found in **Romans 10:9:** "That if you confess with your mouth the Lord Jesus, and believe in your heart that God has raised Him from the dead, you will be saved." This is a crucial piece of information because it tells the listener what he has to do—to first of all believe and then to confess Jesus as Lord. Can you see why witnessing is so important? Because you are not only to believe but you must also tell it, confess it, and bear witness of it. This is confirmed in **Romans 10:13:** "For whoever calls on the name of the Lord shall be saved." Thank God the forgiveness of sins is available to all who dare to trust Jesus as Lord and Savior.

Finally, the apostle then completes the journey by speaking of the benefits of salvation. **Romans 5:1** tells us:

> "Therefore, having being justified by faith, we have peace with God through our Lord Jesus Christ." This is where man finally finds peace and redemption from his sinful nature. Besides, this gives full assurance of our place in the company of the people of God. The journey comes to a magnificent conclusion with Romans 8:1: "There is therefore now no condemnation to those who are in Christ Jesus. Who do not walk according to the flesh but according to the spirit." Can you imagine that? Because of Jesus' death

> on the cross, you can never again be condemned for your sins. Then the apostle capped this off with an incredible promise. which can be found in Romans 8:38–39: "For I am persuaded that neither death nor life, nor angels nor principalities nor powers, nor things present, nor things to come, nor heights, nor depths, nor any other created things shall be able to separate us from the love of God which is in Christ Jesus our Lord."

What an awesome journey this has been. The journey started with a life full of sin and punishable by death and ended with full assurance of life more abundantly. Can you see why you must never be ashamed of the gospel of Christ? It is indeed the power of God unto salvation.

The Romans Road is an easy-to-use tool to understand what your salvation means, and should also be of great help when sharing the clear and easy-to-understand message of the gospel.

Prayer

Prayer should never be underestimated when leading a person to Christ. It is a declaration of that person's reliance on Christ alone for salvation. Keep in mind, however, that it is not the words of the prayer that save them, but the faith behind that prayer.

Following is a simple prayer you can use when leading your prospective convert to the Lord. Have them repeat it after you if they seem uncomfortable doing it alone.

> "Lord, I know that I have sinned against you and am deserving of punishment. But Jesus Christ took the punishment that I deserve so that through faith in Him my sins can be forgiven. With your help, I place my trust in

You for salvation. Thank You for Your wonderful grace and forgiveness—and the gift of eternal life!"

Chapter Checklist.

In review we looked at:

- The process of salvation.
- Why everyone needs salvation.
- How God made the provision for salvation.
- How the unsaved can receive this salvation
- The benefits of obtaining this salvation.

---------------------------------- Questions: ----------------------------------

1. What are the 4 fundamental principles taught in the Book of Romans?

2. Why is the Romans Road to Salvation so important?

3. According to Jesus, there are good people in the world. True/False

4. According to **Romans 3:23**, why does everyone need salvation?

5. What is the penalty for sin according to **Romans 6:23**?

6. All religions lead to God. True/False

7. Unless a person embraces the necessity for Christ's death on the cross, there is no remission of sins. True/False

8. According to **Romans 10:9**, what two words describe how a person can receive salvation?

9. According to **Romans 10:13** who can be saved?

10. How did the apostle Paul complete the journey of salvation? **Romans 5:1**

11. Complete this verse. "There is therefore now no condemnation...

Personal Notes

= CHAPTER TWELVE =

Counting the Cost of Discipleship

Up to this point, I have shared a vast amount of information regarding personal evangelism. For example, I have told you how to conquer fear, how to make that all important initial contact, how to answer difficult questions, how to talk to people from all walks of life including atheists, agnostics, scientists and people from other religions and that's just to name but a few. What I have not told you is that it comes at a price. As it is with anything else, success does not come easily or cheaply. In other words, if you are going to succeed you must be prepared to pay the price.

First, let me remind you that in order to be a witness for Christ, you must be a disciple, period. There is no way you should even consider witnessing for the kingdom until you are a follower of Christ. And to be a disciple of Christ comes with a very high price. In fact, it should cost you your life. Notice the word *should*, because not many people are willing to give up their lives for the gospel. One way or another, you will have to pay with your life. If not physically, you will have to pay spiritually, but you have to die. Let me explain. Jesus said, "Except a grain of wheat falls to the earth and dies, it abides alone." **(John 12:24)** The only way you can be an ambassador for Christ is if you are dead to the flesh and alive in Christ. You cannot be dead to the flesh and be alive in Christ simply by being religious. You need to be a sold-out believer. And it cannot be done for selfish ambition or personal gain.

I grew up hearing people talk about folks being so heavenly-minded they are no earthly good. For me, such a notion is preposterous. In fact, that has to be one of the enemy's biggest deceptions of our day. How can it be possible that one can be so heavenly-minded that he is no earthly good? This kind of mindset is devilish, demonic, and straight from the pit of hell. Certainly, it is not a concept taught in the scriptures and most certainly it could not have come from a spirit-filled believer. If you are someone who believes that you can be too heavenly-minded, let me give you a few scriptures that will eliminate such rubbish from your mind.

- Firstly in **Deuteronomy 6:5–6,** the Bible says this:

"You shall love the LORD your God with all your heart, with all your soul, and with all your strength." Notice that it says "with all,"—not with part, but with all your heart, soul, and strength. Later on in **Mark 12:30**, it reads: "all your heart, all your soul, and all your *mind*." "And these words which I command you today shall be in your heart. You shall teach them diligently to your children, and shall talk of them when you sit in your house, when you walk by the way, when you lie down, and when you rise up."

- **Joshua 1:7-8:**

> "Only be strong and very courageous, that you may observe to do according to all the law which Moses My servant commanded you; do not turn from it to the right hand or to the left, that you may prosper wherever you go. This Book of the Law shall not depart from your mouth, but you shall meditate in it day and night, that you may observe to do according to all that is written in

it. For then you will make your way prosperous, and then you will have good success."

Notice that the Bible says you should meditate upon it "day and night," and in doing so you shall have good success.

- **Isaiah 26:3**

"He will keep in perfect peace whose mind is stayed on Him."

- **Matthew 6:25-33:**

"Therefore I say to you, do not worry about your life, what you will eat or what you will drink; nor about your body, what you will put on. Is not life more than food and the body more than clothing? Look at the birds of the air, for they neither sow nor reap nor gather into barns; yet your heavenly Father feeds them. Are you not of more value than they? Which of you by worrying can add one cubit to his stature? So why do you worry about clothing? Consider the lilies of the field, how they grow: they neither toil nor spin; and yet I say to you that even Solomon in all his glory was not arrayed like one of these. Now if God so clothes the grass of the field, which today is, and tomorrow is thrown into the oven, will He not much more clothe you, O you of little faith? Therefore do not worry, saying, 'What shall we eat?' or 'What shall we drink?' or 'What shall we wear?' For after all these things the Gentiles seek. For your heavenly Father knows that you need all these things.[33] But seek first the kingdom of

God and His righteousness, and all these things shall be added to you."

- **Colossians 3:1-8:**

  "If then you were raised with Christ, seek those things which are above, where Christ is, sitting at the right hand of God. Set your mind on things above, not on things on the earth. For you died, and your life is hidden with Christ in God. When Christ, who is our life, appears, then you also will appear with Him in glory. Therefore, **put to death your members** which are on the earth: fornication, uncleanness, passion, evil desire, and covetousness, which is idolatry. Because of these things the wrath of God is coming upon the sons of disobedience, in which you yourselves once walked when you lived in them. But now you yourselves are to put off all these: anger, wrath, malice, blasphemy, filthy language out of your mouth."

I could go on and on sharing scriptures with you that give credence to the fact that God requires you to give your all. In other words, God requires you to be totally sold out to the kingdom and its principles. God Himself set the example. "For God so loved the world that he gave his *only* Son;" that's why God asked Abraham for his "only son;" that's why Christ gave his all as "a living sacrifice." Friends, can you see why it is a fallacy to suggest that you could become too heavenly-minded? In fact, I believe we should all observe to do as the Scripture says. There is indeed a high price to pay.

12.1 The Cost

As I mentioned earlier every Christian is called to be a disciple of Christ. The problem is, to be a disciple of Christ will cost you everything. It could cost you your family, your loved ones, your friends—basically, it could literally cost you everything. That is what Paul referred to when he said, "I count all things but lost so that I might win Christ." The question is, are you willing and ready to pay the price? Are you ready to give up everything for the excellence of the knowledge of Christ?

In **Matthew 16:24:** Jesus said, "If any man will come after me, let him deny himself, take up his cross and follow me." It means, therefore, that if you want to be a disciple, you must deny yourself, and to deny yourself means to give priority to something or someone over and above your personal needs. For example, you cannot be giving priority to materialism and be sold out to God at the same time. You must remember that it is not about you, it's about Him. This means that Jesus must be given the absolute top priority in your life.

How then will this be orchestrated? By taking up your cross and following Him. In **Luke 9:57-62** we read,

> Now it happened as they journeyed on the road, that someone said to him, "Lord I will follow you wherever you go." And Jesus said to him, "Foxes have holes and birds of the air have nests, but the son of man has nowhere to lay his head." Then he said to another, "Follow me." But he said, "Lord let me first go and bury my father." Jesus said to him, "Let the dead bury their dead, but you go and preach the kingdom of God." And another also said, "Lord I will follow you, *but* let me first go and bid them farewell who are at my house." But Jesus said to him, "No one having put his hand to the plow, and looking back is fit for the kingdom of God."

As you can see from this passage of scripture, it will cost you your very life to be a true disciple of Christ.

Here are some of the things you can expect to suffer, if you are going to become a true disciple of Christ!

- **Shame**

If you are going to become a witness for Christ, you will have to be prepared to suffer shame. Peter said that it was for this very reason we were called. **I Peter 2:21- 24, 4:13** tells us:

"For to this you were called, because Christ also suffered for us, leaving us an example, that you should follow His steps: Who committed no sins, nor was deceit found in His mouth. who, when He was reviled, did not revile in return; when He suffered, He did not threaten, but committed *Himself* to Him who judges righteously; who Himself bore our sins in His own body on the tree, that we, having died to sins, might live for righteousness—by whose stripes you were healed."

Therefore, just as Christ suffered on a cross of shame, we must suffer likewise. To adopt a cliché, "You have to give up to go up." If you are going to master the art of personal evangelism, you have to give up some things that are dear to you. But listen to **1 Peter 4:13-16:**

"But rejoice to the extent that you partake of Christ's sufferings, that when His glory is revealed, you may also be glad with exceeding joy. If you are reproached for the name of Christ, blessed *are you,* for the Spirit of glory and of God rests upon you. On their part He is blasphemed, but on your part He is glorified. But let none of you suffer as a murderer, a thief, an evildoer, or as a busybody in other people's matters. Yet if *anyone suffers* as a Christian, let him not be ashamed, but let him glorify God in this matter."

- **Ridicule**

Not only will you have to suffer shame, but you will also suffer ridicule. This concept is expertly illustrated in **Hebrew 12:2**: "Looking unto Jesus, the author and finisher of our faith, who for the joy that was set before Him endured the cross, despising the shame, and has sat down at the right hand of the throne of God." Notice that it was for "the joy that was set before Him" that He endured the cross. We too must be ready to endure the cross for the joy that awaits us.

- **Rejection**

Remember when I mentioned earlier that the fear of rejection is the greatest stumbling block to witnessing? **1 Peter 2:4** tells us: "Coming to Him as a living stone, rejected indeed by men, but chosen by God and precious." There is no area of your Christian journey where you are more likely to suffer rejection than you will as a witness. However, you can take comfort in knowing that you have been chosen by God and are precious to Him. Even ninety-nine rejections will be worth it when your heart can finally rejoice and the angels can sing seeing one soul come to salvation.

- **Death**

Yes, you may even have to face death for acknowledging Jesus as your Savior. **Acts 10:34-43 says this:**

Then Peter opened his mouth and said:

"In truth I perceive that God shows no partiality. But in every nation whoever fears Him and works righteousness is accepted by Him. The word which God sent to the children of Israel, preaching peace through Jesus Christ—He is Lord of all—that word you know, which

> was proclaimed throughout all Judea, and began from Galilee after the baptism which John preached: how God anointed Jesus of Nazareth with the Holy Spirit and with power, who went about doing good and healing all who were oppressed by the devil, for God was with Him. And we are witnesses of all things which He did both in the land of the Jews and in Jerusalem, whom they killed by hanging on a tree. Him God raised up on the third day, and showed Him openly, not to all the people, but to witnesses chosen before by God, even to us who ate and drank with Him after He arose from the dead. And He commanded us to preach to the people, and to testify that it is He who was ordained by God to be Judge of the living and the dead.'

If you are going to come to that place where you are prepared to suffer shame, ridicule, rejection, and death, you have to make some significant changes in your life, For instance:-

12.2 You Have to Be a New Person

The first change you have to make in your life is you have to exchange your old life for the new because the old cannot inherit the kingdom of God. If you are operating in the flesh, which is the old person, there is no way you are going to appreciate these kind of challenges; therefore, you will need to have adopted the mind of Christ. **2 Corinthians 5:17** says, "Therefore if anyone is in Christ, He is a new creation; old things have passed away; behold, all things are become new." "All things" mentioned here include a change of mindset.

You have to know you are not the person you once were. The old person you used to be is now dead, replaced by a brand new creation. It is only that new person who will be able to endure such hardship.

12.3 Must Put to Death the Deeds of the Flesh

Putting to death the deeds of the old man can only be done once we become brand new and live in the spirit, putting to death our old desires. **1 Peter 4:1–6 says:**

> Therefore, since Christ suffered for us in the flesh, arm yourselves also with the same mind, for he who has suffered in the flesh has ceased from sin, that he no longer should live the rest of his time in the flesh for the lusts of men, but for the will of God. For we have spent enough of our past lifetime in doing the will of the Gentiles—when we walked in lewdness, lusts, drunkenness, revelries, drinking parties, and abominable idolatries. In regard to these, they think it strange that you do not run with them in the same flood of dissipation, speaking evil of you. They will give an account to Him who is ready to judge the living and the dead. For this reason the gospel was preached also to those who are dead, that they might be judged according to men in the flesh, but live according to God in the spirit."

12.4 We Must Abide in Christ

John 15:1–17 tells us:

> "I am the true vine, and my Father is the vinedresser. Every branch in me that does not bear fruit he takes away, and every branch that does bear fruit he prunes, that it may bear more fruit. Already you are clean because of the word that I have spoken to you. Abide in me, and I

in you. As the branch cannot bear fruit by itself, unless it abides in the vine, neither can you, unless you abide in me. I am the vine; you are the branches. Whoever abides in me and I in him, he it is that bears much fruit, for apart from me you can do nothing. If anyone does not abide in me he is thrown away like a branch and withers; and the branches are gathered, thrown into the fire, and burned. If you abide in me, and my words abide in you, ask whatever you wish, and it will be done for you. By this my Father is glorified, that you bear much fruit and so prove to be my disciples. As the Father has loved me, so have I loved you. Abide in my love. If you keep my commandments, you will abide in my love, just as I have kept my Father's commandments and abide in his love. These things I have spoken to you, that my joy may be in you, and that your joy may be full. This is my commandment, that you love one another as I have loved you. Greater love has no one than this, that someone lay down his life for his friends. You are my friends if you do what I command you. No longer do I call you servants, for the servant does not know what his master is doing; but I have called you friends, for all that I have heard from my Father I have made known to you. You did not choose me, but I chose you and appointed you that you should go and bear fruit and that your fruit should abide, so that whatever you ask the Father in my name, he may give it to you. These things I command you, so that you will love one another."

12.5 Are You Prepared to Pay the Price?

The big question you have to ask yourself then is this: Am I prepared, willing, and ready to pay the price of discipleship? One of the reasons more of us are not actively involved in the mission field is simply because we are not prepared to pay the price. What are you willing to give up, to go up? Are you willing to sacrifice that relationship? Are you willing to get rid of those material things you hold dear that are preventing you from being effective in your walk with God? Are you willing to be transformed into the image of Christ? You must be prepared to pay the price.

Chapter Checklist.

In review:

- You must be prepared to pay the price.
- To be a true witness you must first be a true disciple.
- To be a true disciple you have to be dead to the things of the flesh.
- There is a price to be paid for discipleship; it will ultimately cost you everything.
- You must make changes in your personal life if you are going to be willing to suffer.

-------------------------------- Questions: ----------------------------------

1. What is it that you have to be in order to become a witness/ ambassador?

2. Complete the following sentence: The only way you can become an ambassador for Christ is...

3. Name four scriptures that prove you cannot be too heavenly minded!

4. What did the Bible say that God gave to prove that we too need to give our all?

5. What could becoming a disciple of Christ cost you apart from your life?

6. Complete the following Bible verse: If anyone will come after Me...

7. What can a witness for Christ expect to suffer?

8. What significant changes you will be required to make, if you are going to be willing to suffer?

Personal Notes

= CHAPTER THIRTEEN =

Conclusion—Do's and Don'ts/ Conditions for Success

Summary of Main Points

For ease of reference, I cannot think of a better way to send you on your soul winning journey than to remind you of a few crucial points we've covered in the previous twelve chapters, along with the do's and don'ts.

First I would like to remind you that, "God has called you out of darkness into his marvelous light, you are a witness of that light." It is therefore up to you to, "Let your light so shine before men that they may see your good works and glorify your Father which is in heaven." Bearing witness of that light is not as difficult as it may appear to be.

You already possess the necessary basic skills and the knowledge required to accomplish the task. But now you must "study to show yourself approved unto God, a workman that needs not be ashamed rightly dividing the word of truth."

As a representative of the kingdom of God you must behave with diplomacy and distinction.

Probably most importantly, if you are going to master the art of personal evangelism, you must have a desire to do it.

It is the duty of every believer, and not just the titled and gifted to participate in the winning of souls for the kingdom. **(See John 15:16; Matthew 28:19–20.)**

It is God's desire and plan that everyone should be saved. (**See 2 Peter 3:9.**)

Remember that people can only be reached through other people with the exception of the times the Holy Spirit does it Himself.

13.1 Thing you should never do.

Never assume the attitude that you know it all

- o Never be afraid of anyone, "For God has not given you a spirit of fear but of power and of love and of a sound mind."
- o Never lose your cool or become impatient. (You must keep a cool head even in the face of severe opposition.)
- o Never enter into religious mudslinging with anyone; this is not the Clash of the Titans, and you have nothing to prove.
- o Never become too personal, especially, when dealing with the opposite sex.
- o Don't place any confidence in your own personal ability.
- o Don't interrupt others as this may come across as rude.
- o Never enter into doctrinal debates.
- o Try not to come on as too overbearing.
- o Don't get too hung up on results. Leave the increase to God.
- o Be sure not to predetermine or judge anyone because of their lifestyle. Remember, God desires the salvation of all people, and that includes the vilest of sinners.

13.2 Things you must do.

1. You Must Give Yourself Time to Develop Your Skills

The very first thing you must do is, give yourself time to develop your shills. Like a weightlifter, the more weight you lift the stronger and better and more confident you will become. This means, the more you witness, the more proficient you will be.

2. You Must Purpose in Your Heart to Reach the Lost

Like anything else, if you are going to succeed at personal evangelism, you will have to be very practical about it. That means you need to sit down and make a plan of action. "Write the vision and make it plain," because, "without a vision the people perish." You must not only write down your action plan, but you must work to meet the goals of that plan concerning how to reach the lost.

3. You Must Show Yourself Friendly

It is far more effective to reach someone with the gospel by showing that you care about them and their personal well-being, rather than bombarding them with religious arguments. In other words, you should develop genuine friendship, and show people that you care. Do this irrespective of who they may be and/or their lifestyle of choice; it is the soul you are interested in and nothing else. The only way to have a real impact on the unbeliever is to win their confidence with genuine love and friendship.

4. You Must Be Authentic

It is of paramount importance that you are authentic and genuine. If you pretend to be "holier than thou," no one will take you seriously. Believe it or not, people prefer to deal with your flaws than your pretences. It cannot be overemphasized that you live a life that reflects credibility. For instance, "Let your word be your bond." Whatever you do, don't make promises you don't plan to fulfill. Should you make a promise and find you cannot fulfill your obligation, make sure you call to let the individual know; your integrity will be at stake if you don't.

5. **You Must Be a Faithful Servant of the Lord**

   Let faithfulness become your partner so that at the end He will say, "Well done, thou good and faithful servant."—if you are faithful over little, He will make you ruler over much. Therefore, live your life in demonstration of faithfulness to God. Notice that the scripture did not say "Well done, thou good and anointed one," or "Well done, thou good and hard worker." Most of us embrace those things more that we do that which really matters, and that is to be a faithful servant of the Most High God.

Conditions for Success

If you are going to become a successful witness, there are some basic but vital conditions that you will have to meet in order to do so. These are as follows:

1. **You Must Have a Personal Experience of Salvation.**

   According to **John 15:4–5**, Jesus said, "Abide in Me, and I in you. As the branch cannot bear fruit of itself, unless it abides in the vine, neither can you, unless you abide in Me. I am the vine, you are the branches. He who abides in Me, and I in him, bears much fruit; for without Me you can do nothing."

2. **You Must Be an Honorable Vessel, Fit for the Master's use.**

   You will have to live an exemplary life. In his instruction to Timothy, Paul admonished:

   > "Nevertheless the solid foundation of God stands, having this seal: 'The Lord knows those who are His,' and, 'Let everyone who names the name of Christ depart from iniquity.' But in a great house

> there are not only vessels of gold and silver, but also of wood and clay, some for honor and some for dishonor. Therefore if anyone cleanses himself from the latter, he will be a vessel for honor, sanctified and useful for the Master, prepared for every good work" **(2 Timothy 2:19–21).**

To be a vessel of honor, you must therefore be clean, fit for the Master's use.

3. **You Must Have a Keen Interest and Love for the Word**

   The apostle Paul also instructed Timothy to "be diligent to present yourself approved to God, a worker who does not need to be ashamed, rightly dividing the word of truth" **(2 Timothy 2:15).** You must possess a keen interest and love for the Word of God.

4. **You Must Lead a Life of Prayer and Worship**

   It is of vital importance that you spend quality time in the presence of the Lord. Living godly is a life-transforming experience that can be developed during your time of devotion. This is also where your requests can be made known unto God. "And whatever things you ask in prayer, believing, you will receive" **(Matthew 21:22).**

   We should adopt a lifestyle of worship because it is a sure way of getting God's attention to say nothing of the fact that we owe Him our undying devotion. "God inhabits the praises of His people." This means God will visit you via your times of sincere worship.

5. **You Must Possess a Burden and a Passion for Souls**

    In his letter to the Romans, Paul expressed this very thought when he said, "Brethren, my heart's desire and prayer to God for Israel is that they might be saved" (**Romans 10:1**). It should be your heart's desire to see the kingdom of God propagated with the gospel of Jesus Christ so that many should be brought into the kingdom.

Perseverance is the Key.

    Perseverance will unquestionably be one of the most important keys to your success as a witness. As I said earlier, you should not place too much emphasis on the immediate outcome of your witnessing; your objective is to sow seeds rather than to determine how they grow. If you do not get a positive response, don't worry about it. Here is how Paul explains it to the Church in Galatia: "And let us not grow weary while doing good for in due season we will reap if we do not lose heart" **(Galatians 6:9).**

May you experience the awesome presence of the Shekinah each and every time you stand to represent the kingdom as an ambassador for Christ.

Answers to Questions

Chapter 1

1. False
2. To be witnesses unto Him.
3. 80%
4. 95%
5. Reasons for the lack of enthusiasm are as follows:
   i. Lack of awareness
   ii. Feeling of unworthiness and/or guilt
   iii. Ashamed to be identified with Christ
   iv. Unaware of the urgency to reach the world for Christ
   v. Lack of preparation
   vi. Lack of conviction
   vii. Don't know how to witness

6. False.
7. Romans 10:14-17
8. Because of their past.
9. Accusation.
10. Your testimony.
11. The time for harvest is now.
12. 1%
13. Because of society's achievements.
14. True

Chapter 2

1. General and specific.
2. Lack of knowledge, and not knowing our purpose as witnesses.
3. An individual call.
4. A call that is for everyone.
5. Do not believe they are called; Do not have a burden for souls, and; Lack of know how.
6. Listen to hear what God is saying.
7. To be a good listener.
8. He hears the voice of God
9. Write the vision and make it plain
10. A call to holiness
11. Not to strive about words without knowledge
12. With simplicity.
13. That their faith should not be in the wisdom of men, but in the knowledge of God.
14. He will reject us from being priests for Him.

Chapter 3

1. An ambassador.
2. A representative of a particular country to other nations
3. False
4. With diplomacy and distinction.
5. Diplomacy, maintain good relationship between countries.
6. To maintain good relations between the heavenly and the earthly kingdoms.
7. When in trouble in a foreign country.
8. To help someone get into the kingdom of God.
9. As Christ's ambassadors.
10. Excellent communicators, great problem-solving skills, pleasant personality, builders of relationships between their own country and other nations, focus on the one with whom they are communicating, get their message across as clearly as possible.

11. Diplomacy, professional attitude, not short-tempered, not argumentative and take time and get information right before responding to disagreement.

Chapter 4.

1. To rescue the soul from destruction, to tell of the good news of salvation, to testify of what they know about Jesus and to carry out the command of Christ.
2. The wisdom of God in a mystery.
3. Ways Paul acted when he preached to the Corinthians:
    i. He resolved to *know* nothing among them but Jesus Christ and Him crucified—not theology, not philosophy, not science, and not worldly wisdom.
    ii. He purposed in his heart to *make a show* of no other knowledge than that of Christ.
    iii. He determined to *preach* nothing but Christ and Him crucified.
    iv. He was determined to pursue nothing but Jesus Christ. I have read a commentary on this which stated that "Christ in His person and offices, is the sum and substance of the gospel." This then ought to be the subject of any preaching or witnessing. This is powerful stuff.

4. Reasons why we witness:
    i. Because the message of salvation is good news
    ii. To testify of what we know about Jesus
    iii. Because Jesus commanded us to do so

5. False.
6. False.
7. False.
8. True.
9. False.
10. True.

11. That their faith should not stand in the wisdom of men, but in the power of God.
12. False

Chapter 5

1. By possessing knowledge or skill in a particular subject.
2. No.
3. The spirit of a servant.
4. A judgmental spirit.
5. To help the lost experience the love of Christ.
6. To go into the entire world, and preach the gospel.
7. He will be with us always even unto the end of the world.
8. To receive power.

Chapters 6

1. <u>Ways to prepare yourself for witness are:</u>
    i. Have to want to do it.
    ii. Must be a student of the word.
    iii. Must be available.
    iv. Must set a good example.
    v. Should never be ashamed of the gospel.
    vi. Must stay in control.
    vii. Must take it outside your own community
    viii. Must be determined and persistent and
    ix. Will need spiritual wisdom.

2. Doctrinal debates.
3. To bring faith, conviction and salvation into the lives of unbelievers.
4. Excuses.
5. Choose softer targets.
6. Your example.
7. 1% aspiration, 99% perspiration.
8. Opportunity.
9. Spiritual wisdom.

Chapter 7

1. Fear.
2. Fear of rejection and Peer pressure.
3. False Evidence Appearing Real.
4. Let nobody's opinion of you become your reality
5. <u>Ways fear is likely to affect you:</u>
    - i. Will prevent you from being effective.
    - ii. Will affect your behavior.
    - iii. Will affect your confidence.
    - iv. will prevent you from functioning with courage.
    - v. Will prevent you from speaking out.
    - vi. Will cause you to lack the ability and the capacity to function different from others.
6. Those who care and those who will exploit you.
7. A spirit of fear.
8. Take your rejection as a challenge.

Chapter 8

1. <u>Three basic rules for how to initiate contact:</u>
    - i. Change your language.
    - ii. Choose your targets.
    - iii. Find a need and fill it.
2. The Good Samaritan.
3. The one that showed mercy on him.
4. Guide answer, that you are being a neighbor to those who you have mercy.
5. Go and do likewise.
6. To preach the kingdom of God.
7. Power and authority.
8. False.
9. False.
10. That you are interested in the person and to establish a common ground.

11. Water.
12. By simply asking for a drink.

Chapter 9

1. Greek philosophy and Jewish legalism.
2. The love for knowledge.
3. The Holy Spirit.
4. He will tell you what to say in that hour.
5. The Bible.
6. Not to be ashamed of the gospel because it was the power of God or rightly dividing the word of truth.
7. That proper Bible study leads to approval from God.
8. Doctrine, reproof, correction, instruction in righteousness.
9. Honesty.
10. The burden of proof is on them, not you.
11. Help to divert attention.

Chapter 10

1. <u>Reasons why it is difficult to witness to religious Christians are that:</u>
    i. They know the Bible
    ii. They know about God
    iii. They think they are good people, and
    iv. Doctrinal influence.

2. Sectarianism.
3. False.
4. Luke 9:49-50.
5. You will get into conflicts.
6. The conscience.
7. Praise reports/testimony.
8. <u>The other two ways to witness to people you know are:</u>
    i. Give them a point of reference
    ii. Use the first person approach.

9. Care, understanding and skill.
10. False.
11. The burden of proof is with anyone who says there is no God.
12. Mohammed.
13. The Quran.
14. The Torah, the Zabur and the Injeel.
15. <u>Things Muslims think about Jesus:</u>
    i. That He was born of a virgin
    ii. Was a great prophet,
    iii. Not a God but only a man,
    iv. Jesus spoke as a baby,
    v. Heal the sick,
    vi. raise the dead
    vii. The breath of God
    viii. The spirit of God
    ix. The life of God, The Word of God
    x. Do not think Jesus died on the cross
    xi. God took Him before He was crucified
    xii. He will return to usher in the final judgment.

16. By performing the five pillars of faith.
17. No. (They believe that their works will be accounted on the Day of Judgment.)

Chapter 11

1. <u>The four fundamental principles taught in the Book of Romans are:</u>
    i. Why everyone needs salvation
    ii. How God made the provision for salvation!
    iii. How we can receive that salvation, and;
    iv. The benefits of obtaining salvation

2. Because some people believe they are good people and do not need salvation.
3. False

4. Because all have sinned.
5. Death
6. False
7. True
8. Believe and confess.
9. Whosoever shall call on the name of the Lord.
10. Being justified by faith we have peace with God.
11. To those who are in Christ.

Chapter 12

1. A disciple of Christ.
2. If you are dead to the flesh and alive in Christ.
3. Deuteronomy 6:5-6, Joshua 1:7, Matthew 6:25-33 and Ephesians 3:1-8.
4. His only begotten Son.
5. Your family, your love ones and your friends.
6. Let him deny himself, take up his cross and follow me.
7. Shame, ridicule, rejection and death.
8. <u>The significant changes you will be required to make, if you are going to be willing to suffer for Christ are:</u>
   i. Have to be a new person.
   ii. Have to put to death the deeds of the flesh.
   iii. Have to abide in Christ.

References

Release International—the voice for persecuted Christian

New Spirit Filled Life Bible (NKJV) http://www.lillyofthevalley.com/Jesuslovesyou—godsnames—complist.html.

The Comprehensive Commentary of the Bible—Matthew Henry, Thomas Scott

Five Great Dialog Classic Club Edition, **1969,P.93.**

William S. Sahakiam—History of Philosophy, **1968,P.56.**

University of Washington, History of Ancient Philosophy) **(414a20ff).**

The Webster's Dictionary

The Merriam Webster's Dictionary

http://EzineArticles.com/?expert=Winnifred Anderson—Your Role as an Ambassador for Christ

Christianity Magazin.co.uk—July 2011—The Evangelism Issue

http://www.biblebb.com/files/mac/**53-14.**htm—John MacArthur

http://bible.com/bibleanswers_result.php?=**113**

http://www.overcomepanic.com—Christian Help for Anxiety

http:/carm.org/dos-and-don'ts-of-witnessing

http://www.invitationtochrist.org/witness.htm

http://christiananswers.net/evangelism/belief/atheism.html

Auto Biography

Glen Kerr is an ordained pastor and founder of Pneuma Life Transformation Ministries Intl. (Currently, a church without walls ministry). A longtime qualified financial professional, he is a graduate of the London Guildhall University and the Brixton Bible Institute London UK respectively. Post graduate studies in Accountancy (Chartered Association of Certified Accountants) ACCA, Association of Accounting Technicians (MAAT) and an honorary MBA. Pastor Kerr has been a Christian for over 35 years and has served in numerous church positions. He has a clear apostolic anointing on his life, confirmed both by words of prophecy and a powerful demonstration to that effect. His ministry has taken him around the world in an ongoing effort to empower the Body of Christ and to win souls for the kingdom. He lives in the UK.

CPSIA information can be obtained at www.ICGtesting.com
Printed in the USA
LVOW08s1105061113

360239LV00001B/70/P